Introduction

Early childhood professionals know that children are active learners and understand the many benefits of physical activity and play, including the contributions of both to the cognitive domain. They understand that young children are experiential learners, and that the more senses used in the learning process, the more children retain (Fauth, 1990). Gardner's (1993) recognition of bodily/kinesthetic intelligence validated the use of the whole body and parts of the body as a way of learning and knowing. Brain research confirms that the mind and body are not separate entities and that the functions of the body contribute to the functions of the mind.

With the recent clamor for more accountability and testing—and the emphasis placed almost exclusively on early literacy—seatwork is once again threatening to supplant active learning. Even physical education and recess are being eliminated in favor of more "academic time." This is indeed ironic in an age when there has never been greater concern about childhood obesity. As a result, teachers feel pressured to teach young children in ways they know are developmentally inappropriate.

Children, however, haven't changed. They still need to experience concepts physically to fully understand them, including concepts that fall under the heading of literacy and language arts. Teachers are quite aware of this, and are frustrated at being asked to "teach" literacy with flashcards, drills, and worksheets.

Emergent Literacy—Then and Now

Throughout the years, teachers have used different methods and forms to develop children's literacy. For a long time, educators (and policy makers) debated the wisdom of emphasizing phonics and word recognition rather than whole language, which puts the child's language experience into meaningful context. Today, educators are likely to blend the two approaches. Whether we refer to the child's process of becoming a fully literate person as the study of *language arts* or, more recently, as *emergent literacy*, the components remain the same: listening, speaking, reading, and writing.

These four components are about *communication*—sent and received—which means that they play a vital role in every individual's life. The study of language arts is part of every curriculum, in one form or another, from preschool through advanced education. It is tied to linguistic intelligence, which is granted enormous respect in our society.

In early childhood programs, language arts have traditionally received the greatest concentration during daily group or circle times. During these periods, teachers or caregivers read stories or poems to the children who sit and listen. Often, discussion precedes or follows the readings. In elementary schools, reading and writing have too commonly been handled as separate studies, with the children focusing on individual topics like phonics, spelling, and grammar.

Today's approach to children's emergent literacy recognizes that listening, speaking, reading, and writing overlap and interrelate, each contributing to the growth of the others. This approach acknowledges that children learn best those concepts that are relevant to them. Language acquisition and development must be a natural process that occurs over time, relates to all aspects of a child's life, and actively involves the child in making meaning (Sawyer & Sawyer, 1993; Raines & Canady, 1990).

The Rationale for Active Learning in Literacy

Research demonstrates that movement is the young child's preferred mode of learning, and that children learn best through active involvement (Hannaford, 1995).

For example, prepositions—those little words so critical to language and life—are very much a part of physical experiences. As children move *over, under, around, through, beside,* and *near* objects (for example, *under* the monkey bars, *through* the tunnel, *over* the balance beam), these words take on greater significance.

Olds (1994) writes that such spatial orientation is necessary for letter identification and the orientation of symbols on a page. She explains that a lowercase *b* and a lowercase *d*, for example, are the same, both composed of a line and a circle. The only difference is in their spatial orientation—which side of the line the circle is on. When children take on the straight and curving lines of letters with their bodies and body parts rather than simply attempting to copy them on paper from a chart on the wall, their sense of directionality and spatial orientation is greatly enhanced.

Block (2001, p. 44) contends that sequencing movement "accesses many learning modes." She recommends that children have opportunities to listen to the rhythm of language and to actively participate in physical expressions of its rhythm. For example, tapping to the rhythm of children's rhymes and poems develops temporal awareness. And that, Block says, creates an awareness of the rhythm of literary works and helps children later "internalize the beat when they are being read to."

Stringing actions together to form sequences (and eventually dances or athletic activities) is similar to linking words to form sentences and eventually paragraphs. Both require that children choose components that flow naturally. Both require breathing room (a pause in the action, or a comma) and an ending (a full stop, or a period).

When children learn, create, or dance to songs, they experience flow and phrasing. When the songs have lyrics, children must ponder the meanings of words. And because those words are important to them, they have much more relevance than a vocabulary list or a spelling list.

When children perform a "slow" walk or skip "lightly," adjectives and adverbs become much more than abstract concepts. When they are given the opportunity to demonstrate physically action words such as *stomp, pounce, stalk,* or *slither* or descriptive words such as *smooth, strong, gentle,* or *enormous,* word comprehension is immediate and long-lasting. Even suffixes take on greater relevance when children act out the difference between *scared* and *scary.* (Try it yourself and see how vivid the difference is!) In all of these instances, the children have heard the word and both felt and seen the meaning.

When children speak and listen to one another, such as when they invent games on the playground, they are using and expanding their vocabularies and learning important lessons in communication. When they invent rules for those games, as young children like to do, they enhance their communication skills. Talking about experiences, depicting them through actions, and then discussing the actions all contribute to language development by requiring children to make essential connections among their cognitive, social/emotional, and physical domains. We know that when young children learn something in one domain, it has an impact on the other domains.

Jensen (2001) labels this kind of active learning *implicit,* like learning to ride a bike. At the opposite end of the spectrum is *explicit* learning, like being told the capital of Peru. To explain the difference, Jensen asks, if you had not ridden a bike in five years, would you still be able to do it? And if you had not heard the capital of Peru for five years, would you remember it?

Explicit learning may be quicker than learning through physical experience, but the latter has greater meaning for children and stays with them longer. There are many reasons for this, including the fact that implicit learning creates more neural networks in the brain and employs more senses. Another reason may be that it is simply more fun!

What Movement, Music, and Literacy Have in Common

Teachers in preschool through the early elementary grades often say that they do not have time to include movement and music in their curriculum. There are standards to be met and tests to be taken—primarily in the area of literacy—and movement and music are increasingly viewed as frills. Teachers and children alike lament the loss of two of the most popular classroom subjects.

But they do not have to lose movement and music! Of course, it may no longer be acceptable to run, jump, and sing in the classroom just for the joy and the physical and social/emotional benefits of it. But what if movement and music have cognitive benefits? What if they can be used to help children meet literacy standards and pass standardized tests? What if the notion that movement/music and emergent literacy are mutually exclusive is just plain incorrect?

The fact is, movement and music are essential to active learning; and movement, music, and the language arts are linked naturally.

Movement and music, like language, are forms of communication and self-expression. Body language is a distinct method of communication, and it is believed that "ideas and feelings expressed in words actually begin in the body….Before you write or speak, there is a physical response in the body" (Minton, 2003, p. 37). Studies have shown that our bodies express more than our words during communication with others. Doubters should stand before a group of people and say, "Put your hands over your eyes," while actually placing hands over the ears to test this theory. The vast majority of the group will mimic the leader's actions and will stand with their hands over their ears!

Music is part of every culture. Indeed, many feel that music is the universal language. Studies have shown that children exposed to music have greater motivation to communicate with others.

Rhythm is an essential part of language arts, movement, and music. While we may think of rhythm primarily in musical terms, there is a rhythm to words and sentences. We develop an internal rhythm when we read and write. Individuals have personalized rhythms for thinking and moving. When a teacher asks a class of children to get into small body shapes, for example, the children each respond at their own pace, some quickly and some slowly. Moreover, as children acquire and refine their motor skills, they learn subconscious lessons about rhythm. For example, a gallop matches a 2/4 musical meter. A walk is similar to a 4/4 meter. And a skip has the feel of a 6/8.

Music is vital to language and listening skills. (It is inconceivable that anyone could contest this!) Music activities improve attention span, expand vocabulary, and enhance memory. None of us would have learned our ABCs so quickly if it were not for "The Alphabet Song!" Music activities promote active listening, a core component of communication, and one sadly lacking in most communication! And, of course, Gardner (1993) has identified musical intelligence as yet another way of learning and knowing.

According to Coulter (1995, p. 22), songs, movement, and musical games are "brilliant neurological exercises" vital to intellectual development. She states that by combining rhythmic movement with speech and song, young children are given an opportunity to further develop their minds, particularly in the areas of "inner speech" and "impulse control," which contribute to language development, self-management, and social skills.

Movement, music, and language are abstract, consisting as they do of symbols and ideas. But when the three are used in combination, abstract concepts suddenly become concrete. The word "slow," for example, has only so much meaning to a child when she reads it or spells it. When she actually hears slow music, the meaning is expanded. And when she moves to slow music, the meaning is definitive in both mind and body.

How to Use This Book

The activities in *Jump into Literacy* offer children opportunities to experience physically and fully, through their bodies and their voices, concepts that fall under the four components of language arts: listening, speaking, reading, and writing. These components make up the four main sections of this book.

Every activity in the book has at least two headings: "To Have" and "To Do." Each activity begins with information on the activity's role in emergent literacy and anything you should pass on to the children before starting. The "To Have" section lists materials needed for the activity. (Most require no materials or optional materials.) The "To Do" section describes how to do the activity. If an activity has extensions, they are listed under "More to Do." And if there is children's literature or music relevant to the activity, it is included along with an identifying icon—a book for literature and a musical note for recordings—to make them easy to identify. You can use these books and recordings to extend the children's learning.

The four chapters of the book—beginning with listening, then speaking, then reading, and finally writing—appear in developmental order, from least to most challenging. To the best of my ability, I have arranged the activities within each chapter according to level of difficulty. The activities are not meant to be used one after the other in the order in which they appear in the book, and they do not progress in a neat, step-by-step sequence, from Point A to Point Z because children do not learn in that manner. There is considerable interrelatedness among the four areas of listening, speaking, reading, and writing, and children acquire knowledge in overlapping ways.

I suggest that you begin with the simplest activities in Chapter 1: Listening, repeating them for as long as the children remain interested. It is likely that you will tire of the activities long before the children do, but that's okay. Repetition is essential to reinforcing learning in early childhood! Skip and mark those extensions that are too challenging for the children. Then move on to the simplest activities in Chapter 2: Speaking. Continue in this manner, letting the children's interest, abilities, and enthusiasm for the material guide you to when it is time to move on. When activities are too simple for them, they will become bored. When activities are too difficult for them, they will become frustrated. Continue with Chapter 3: Reading and Chapter 4: Writing.

When you have completed all of the activities the children are capable of doing in each of the four chapter, return to Chapter 1: Listening. Repeat any activities that you feel need reinforcing. For those with extensions, you should repeat the initial activity and then try the extension. Once again, let the children's interest, abilities, and enthusiasm guide you to when it is time to move on to Chapter 2: Speaking, repeating and extending as you see fit. Continue with Chapter 3: Reading and Chapter 4: Writing.

Whether you use these activities during circle or group time, substitute them for more traditional lessons in language arts, or use them as follow-ups to your curriculum or theme lessons, you can be sure that the children will move in leaps and bounds toward becoming capable listeners, speakers, readers, and writers. Moreover, because you are teaching the *whole child,* using the physical and social/emotional, as well as the cognitive, you can be sure that the lessons learned will be long lasting and meaningful.

CHAPTER 1

Listening

Language is either given or received. For communication to be effective, the individual on the receiving end must have the ability to listen well, which is a learned skill.

Listening well is also essential for learning to speak and read skillfully. Machado (2003, p. 237) tells us that children must be able to hear the sounds of language (phonological awareness), separate from its meaning. Children should understand that "language can be analyzed into strings of separate words and that words can be analyzed in sequences of syllables and phonemes within syllables…." She explains that many children who have difficulty learning to read cannot hear the sequences of sounds in words.

The California Department of Education (1999) published *First Class*, a set of developmentally appropriate guidelines for teaching language skills in preschool through first grade. The first guideline states that experiences should help develop positive feelings toward learning "through" a sense of playfulness and fun.

The activities in this chapter promote:

- *active listening*
- *auditory discrimination* (the ability to distinguish among sounds)
- *auditory sequential memory* (the ability to hear and recall a series of words, sounds, or instructions)
- *phonological awareness* (an appreciation for the sounds and meaning of spoken words)
- *phonemic awareness* (an awareness that language is broken down into small units called phonemes, which correspond to the letters of the alphabet).

And although it all sounds like serious business (which it is), you can be sure the children will still have plenty of fun with it!

Develops auditory discrimination

What Do You Hear?

In this simple activity, children identify sounds.

To Have

Objects with familiar sounds (keys on a keychain, a whistle, a bell, and so on)

To Do

● The children close their eyes.
● Make a sound, and ask the children to identify it. Some sounds to try are rattling a keychain, clapping your hands, ringing a bell, opening and closing a drawer, or blowing a whistle. Identifying sounds with eyes closed requires careful listening!

More to Do

● A more difficult challenge is use a tape recorder to record familiar sounds children might hear both in and out of the classroom. Possibilities include a vacuum cleaner, a door closing, a phone ringing, a clock ticking, an electric can opener, or a doorbell.
● Invite the children to demonstrate each object on the tape either by pretending to be the object or pretending to use it. For example, if one of the sounds is a vacuum cleaner, the child can act like a vacuum cleaner or pretend she is vacuuming.

A TICKING CLOCK

PRETENDING to be a VACUUM

Ella Jenkins' *And One and Two* was designed to help preschoolers and kindergarteners develop their listening skills. Also, Melody House's *El Mundo del Sonido (The World of Sound)* consists of some 70 sounds. There is a three-second pause between each sound, which makes it easy to pause the recording to allow the children to guess what they heard. The origin of the sound is then given, first in Spanish and then in English.

A Listening Walk

The benefits of this activity are numerous, as it combines experiences in all three developmental domains: physical (a walk outside: moving), social/emotional (a feeling of belonging and an appreciation for nature and the community: feeling), and cognitive (the promotion of listening skills and auditory discrimination: thinking).

To Have

No materials needed

To Do

- Explain to the children that they are going outside on a listening walk to discover how many things they can hear. Remind them to put on their "listening ears" and to move very quietly.
- Take the children for at least a 10-minute walk. When you get back to the classroom, ask them to describe the things they heard.

More to Do

- Bring a small tape recorder with you to capture sounds the children hear. Play the recording in the classroom and challenge the children to identify the sounds.
- The children portray each object identified, either by taking on its shape or by performing its movement. For example, upon hearing leaves rustling in the breeze, one child might form the shape of a leaf with her body or body parts. Another child might pretend to be a leaf shaking in the wind.

The Listening Walk by Paul Showers is the perfect accompaniment to these activities.

Promotes auditory discrimination

Head, Shoulders, Knees, and Toes

This timeless favorite is probably best known as a body-part identification activity, but it is also about auditory discrimination.

To Have

No materials needed

To Do

- The children touch the corresponding part of their bodies (head, shoulders, knees, and toes) as you call out each part, first in the order in which it appears in the title of the song and then in varying orders (for example, toes, knees, shoulders, and head; or shoulders, toes, head, and knees).
- Pause before naming each body part so the children never know what is coming next or when it is coming!

More to Do

- Increase and decrease the speed at which you call out the body parts to introduce children to the *tempo* of sounds (related to speech patterns). This requires careful listening.

If you want to use a recorded version of the song, play "Head, Shoulders, Knees, and Toes" on Hap Palmer's *Early Childhood Classics—Old Favorites with a New Twist* CD.

Simon Says

Simon Says is a listening activity. Play it without the elimination process to promote active listening with all the children.

To Have

No materials needed

To Do

- Arrange the children in two circles or lines.
- Call out commands to the children, beginning most commands with the words, "Simon says." When the children hear those words, they are to perform the requested action. For example, "Simon says, 'Place your hands on your head'" or "Simon says, 'Place your hands on your hips.'" When you do not say, "Simon says," the children do not do the action. If children do the action anyway, they move from their circle or line to the other circle or line and continue to play.
- The children will need to listen carefully for the phrase "Simon says" to know whether they follow the direction or not.

Use musical versions of the game for a greater challenge. Frank Leto's *Move Your Dancing Feet* includes "Simon Says"; Maryann "Mar" Harman's *Playing and Learning with Music* offers "Simple Simon Says."

Follow up with a fun literary twist on the game by reading *Simon Says!* by Shen Roddie.

Encourages active listening

Where Is It Coming From?

This active listening exercise requires that children determine where a sound is coming from.

To Have

An object with which to make a sound (bell, tambourine, or maraca)

BELLS

To Do

- Have the children stand throughout the room with their eyes closed.
- Tiptoe to one part of the room and make a sound with one object.
- The children (eyes closed!) turn and point to where the sound is coming from. Invite them to open their eyes to reorient themselves and to determine whether or not they guessed correctly.
- Have them close their eyes again as you tiptoe to a different area of the room and make the sound again.

Read *My Five Senses* by Aliki and initiate a discussion about hearing, as well as the other four senses.

Who Said That?

This exercise in auditory discrimination will work best after the children have been together for a while and can recognize one another's voices. While the previous activity (Where Is It Coming From?) requires children to determine where a sound is coming from, this one asks them to determine where and who it is coming from!

To Have

No materials needed

To Do

- The children spread out around the room, and then stand with their eyes closed.
- Tiptoe to one child and tap her on the shoulder. When you tap her on the shoulder, she opens her eyes and does not speak.
- After you move to the center of the room silently motion to the selected child to speak aloud a few predetermined words, such as, "Mary had a little lamb."
- The rest of the children open their eyes, point to the child whom they believe was speaking, and say her name aloud.
- Then have them close their eyes again for another round.

The Very Quiet Cricket by Eric Carle is all about sound. Read it aloud to inspire further discussion on the topic.

Promotes the ability to discriminate between sound and silence

Statues

This musical game helps children differentiate between sound and silence while also providing experience with rhythm, tempo, and volume, all part of the language arts.

To Have

CD or cassette player and recordings of music that inspire movement

To Do

- Explain to the children that they should move while the music is playing and freeze into "statues" when the music stops. Ask them to remain as statues until the music starts again.
- Play the music and then stop and start the music randomly by pressing and releasing the pause button on the tape or CD player.
- Take the children by surprise by varying the amount of time you play and then pause the music. This will require careful listening and patience!

More to Do

- Every time you play this game, use music with a different rhythm. Select different styles of music, such as rock and roll, a waltz, a polka, or a march. Because rhythm is essential to speaking, reading, and writing, this activity provides the children with a lesson in the other language arts as it also promotes active listening.

For added ease, use "The Freeze" from Greg and Steve's *Kids in Motion* when playing the game—it has the pauses built in! Or try "Rock and Roll Freeze Dance" from Hap Palmer's *So Big: Activity Songs for Little Ones*.

Musical Partners

Like Statues (page 20), this is another musical game that helps children discriminate between sound and silence. Children must listen carefully, but they won't mind because they will be having so much fun!

To Have

CD or cassette player and recordings of music that inspire movement

To Do

- Have the children choose partners. Play the music.
- When the music starts, the partners move away from each other in any way they wish.
- When the music stops, they find each other quickly, hold hands, and sit down until the music starts again.

The song "Partners" on *Learning Basic Skills Through Music, Volume 2* by Hap Palmer offers variations on this theme.

Encourages active listening and rhythmic awareness

Pop Goes the Weasel!

Waiting for the "Pop" in this familiar song is an exercise in active listening. Walking to the rest of the song promotes rhythmic awareness.

To Have

Recording of "Pop Goes the Weasel" (optional)

To Do

- Sing or play a recording of "Pop Goes the Weasel."
- The children walk around the room while the music plays and jump into the air every time they hear the "Pop."
- If your space is large enough, the children can walk freely. Otherwise, they should walk in a circle.

More to Do

- If you are singing this song, change the tempo at which you sing it with every round.
- Ask the children to jump and clap with each "Pop." Next, have them jump and change direction with each "Pop."
- Challenge the children to freeze each time they hear "Pop" and not move again until the next verse begins.

Children All-Star Rhythm Hits, by Jack Capon and Rosemary Hallum, includes a version of "Pop Goes the Weasel."

Five Little Monkeys

You can use this chant or song as a fingerplay or simply let the children experience its beat. It is a wonderful listening activity and great for experiencing rhythm and rhyme.

To Have

No materials needed

To Do

- Read each of the following lines, demonstrating the movements suggested in parentheses. Then repeat the process, encouraging the children to perform the actions with you.

Five little monkeys (hold up five fingers)
Jumping on the bed, (move closed fists up and down twice)
One fell off and bumped his head. (hold up one finger; put hand to head)
Mama called the doctor and the doctor said, (mime being on the telephone)
"No more monkeys jumping on the bed." (shake finger "no-no" twice)

Four little monkeys…(hold up four fingers)
Three little monkeys…(hold up three fingers)
Two little monkeys…(hold up two fingers)

One little monkey…(hold up one finger)
(Lines two to four remain the same)
"Get those monkeys back to bed." (extend arm
  and point twice toward "bed")

More to Do

- With repetition, the children will be able to say the words and do the actions simultaneously. This promotes active listening and speaking experience.
- Read the verses with a steady rhythm and ask the children to jump to the rhythm. This allows them to feel the rhythm of the words with their whole body!

You can find a musical version of this song on Maryann "Mar" Harman's *Playing and Learning with Music.*

Develops auditory processing

Up, Up, and Away

Identifying the pitch of a sound is an important part of auditory processing, which, in turn, is essential to language development.

To Have

Slide whistle (optional)

To Do

- Explain the meaning of the words *ascending* (getting higher and higher) and *descending* (getting lower and lower) to the children. Demonstrate the meaning of the words with both your voice (hum or sing a note) and your arms.
- Using either a slide whistle or your voice (hum or sing a note), start with a low note, and gradually go higher and higher.
- The children raise their arms with each *ascending* note.
- Reverse the process, and the children lower their arms on the *descending* notes.

More to Do

- When the children are accustomed to this exercise, have them crouch low to the floor and use their whole bodies to denote the ascending and descending notes.
- Pause occasionally to help the children differentiate between sound and silence.

Listen Closely

This multi-purpose activity requires children to listen beyond the initial sound of words.

To Have

No materials needed

To Do

- Sit on the floor with the children and explain that you are going to say three words that begin with the same sound but that each requires a different action. For example, when you say *sunshine,* they should make a circle above their heads with their arms. When you say *seal,* they should clap their hands in front of them like a seal. And when you say *salute,* they should salute with their hand to their forehead.
- Tell the children the words you've chosen, and demonstrate the accompanying actions.
- Start by saying the words in the same order; eventually mix them up!

More to Do

- To make the game more challenging, occasionally say a word with the same beginning sound but to which you haven't assigned an action. For example, if you've been using *sunshine, seal,* and *salute,* you might suddenly add *silly, soap,* or another word that begins with *s.*
- To focus on the same sound—for example, the /s/ sound—over a period of time, change the words and actions. For example, you might use *soap* (the children pretend to scrub), *sandwich* (the children put their hands together, one palm facing up and the other down), and *sink* (the children slump). To familiarize them with the sound of two consonants together, use words like *smile* (the children smile), *smoke* (the children indicate smoke rising with one or both hands), and *smell* (the children sniff).
- Play this game with words beginning with any letter or combination of letters.

Hap Palmer's *One Little Sound: Fun with Phonics and Numbers* and *Two Little Sounds: Fun with Phonics and Numbers* are a nice complement to the activity.

Listen, Buddy by Helen Lester is an entertaining book about a rabbit with very big ears that is not very good at listening.

Promotes active listening

Gossip

*This simple game enhances children's listening skills. They will have too much
fun to realize that they are also learning!*

To Have

No materials needed

To Do

- Sit in a circle with the children and whisper a word into the ear of the child to
  your right or left.
- Continuing in the same direction, that child then whispers the same word into
  the ear of the child next to her and so on around the circle.
- When the word finally returns to you, say aloud whatever you heard and the
  word that you whispered into the ear of the first child.
- If the two words are different, ask the children how that happened.
- Play the game again with a different child starting every round.

Stand Up/Sit Down

This activity gives children lots of physical and mental exercise at the same time as it promotes careful listening. It also reinforces understanding of the concepts of up and down.

To Have

One chair per child (optional)

To Do

- Have the children sit in chairs or on the floor (although sitting on the floor means that they have much further to go to stand up!).
- Give them instructions to either stand up or sit down. For example:

  - Stand up if you are wearing blue.
  - Sit down if you are a boy.
  - Stand up if you have blond hair.
  - Sit down if you have brown eyes.
  - Stand up if you have a cat at home.
  - Sit down if you have a dog at home.
  - Stand up if you have a bird at home.
  - Sit down if you like chocolate.
  - Stand up if you like vanilla.
  - Sit down if you heard what I said!

Develops phonemic awareness

I Spy

This age-old game requires children to listen carefully and identify beginning sounds, while recognizing that the sounds stand for something.

To Have

No materials needed

To Do

- Tell the children, "I spy something that begins with a /b/ sound."
- The children point to, move to, or touch something that begins with the letter *b*. Repeat with other letters with which they are familiar.

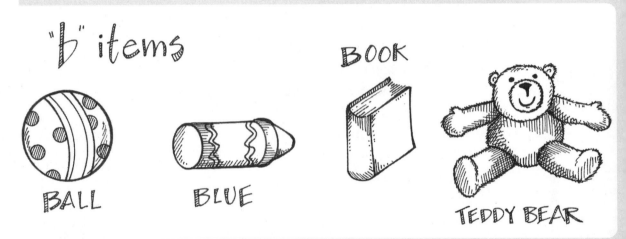

More to Do

- As an alternative, tell the children you spy something "that starts the same way as the word *dog*." This requires that they identify the initial sound themselves.
- Play the game with letter combinations, like *ch*, *st*, or *tr*.
- Use this game to reinforce rhymes; for example, tell the children you spy something that rhymes with *curl*.

"Something That Begins Like" on Hap Palmer's *Learning Basic Skills Through Music, Volume 2* is a great follow-up to these activities.

Marco Polo

You may have played this game as a child. It is a great listening activity because it requires participants to use their sense of hearing.

To Have

A large indoor or outdoor space

To Do

- Choose a child to be "IT" and have her stand at a distance from the rest of the children who must stand with their eyes closed.
- The goal is for the children to find IT using only their listening skills.
- The children who have their eyes closed call out "Marco," to which IT responds "Polo."
- The children continue saying "Marco" and IT continues saying "Polo" in a call-and-response format until one child locates IT. This child becomes the next IT.

More to Do

- The children can play this as a partner game, with one partner trying to find the other. To make it easier to play among a group of children, assign each pair of partners different code words. For example, one pair could be "Marco Polo," another "Christopher Columbus," another "Lewis and Clark," and so on. Or the children can simply use their own first names.
- When the children have had ample experience with each set of partners using different code words, try this with all the sets of partners using "Marco Polo." This will require superior listening skills to achieve voice recognition.

Pass a Rhythm

This game is like Gossip (page 26) except that a beat is passed around the circle rather than a word. In addition to fostering active listening, this game develops a sense of rhythm.

To Have

No materials needed

To Do

- Sit in a circle with the children and clap out a simple rhythm (for example, 1-2) on your lap or on the floor in front of you. Counting the beats aloud at first will help the children succeed.
- The child next to you repeats that rhythm, and the game continues in a similar manner around the circle.
- When it is your turn again, start the game with a different rhythm (for example, 1-2-3). Are the children listening closely enough to repeat accurately what they hear?

More to Do

- Use rhythm sticks rather than hands to add variety to the activity.
- Combine rhythms when the children are ready to move on to something more challenging. For example, you might beat out 1-2, 1-2-3.
- Eventually, the children can take turns choosing rhythms.

Rhythm Stick Activities by Henry Buzz Glass and Rosemary Hallum complements these experiences.

Ducks, Cows, Cats, and Dogs

Before playing this hilarious game, talk to the children about the animals mentioned in the title. What sound does each animal make? If you are playing with very young children or a very small group, choose just two or three animals. If you are playing with older children, or with children who have experienced the original version, add other animals to the mix. Make sure to use animals with familiar sounds, such as chickens, pigs, or sheep.

To Have

No materials needed

To Do

- With the children scattered throughout the room, whisper the name of an animal in each player's ear. Once you have assigned each child an animal, have the children get on their hands and knees and close their eyes.

- When you give them the signal to start, they should begin to move about the room with their eyes still closed, making the sound of each animal and trying to find the other animals that are just like them! Let the children know when all of the cats have found each other, for example. Then they can sit and watch the others who are still trying to find the animals that are like them.

- Closing their eyes will help the children focus on listening; but with so many sounds being made at once, differentiating among them will be a challenge!

To stimulate a discussion about cats and dogs, read *When It Rained Cats and Dogs* by Nancy Bird Turner. Or read *Moozie's Kind Adventure* by Jane Morton—the main character is a cow who befriends the ducks that play near her farm.

Listening   31

Promotes active listening and experiences with rhythm, rhyme, and word comprehension

Fingerplay Folly

Children love familiar fingerplays; they take great pride in knowing all of the words and actions! This activity is great for promoting active listening, Because you are using fingerplays, the children also get all the benefits that fingerplays traditionally offer, including experience with rhythm, rhyme, and word comprehension.

To Have

No materials needed

To Do

- Choose one of the children's favorite familiar fingerplays. Say the rhyme and do the actions with the children. Suggested fingerplays include "Five Little Ducks," "Here Is a Beehive," "Ten in the Bed," "Two Little Blackbirds," and "Where Is Thumbkin?"
- While continuing to do the actions, eliminate first one line and then additional lines from the fingerplay, testing the children's memory and listening skills. Do they know what was missing?

More to Do

- Say a line incorrectly. If the children have been listening carefully, they will be happy to point out your mistake!

Finger Frolics and *Finger Frolics 2* by Liz Cromwell offer many fingerplays. There are also plenty of fingerplays to choose from in *The Complete Book of Rhymes, Songs, Poems, Fingerplays, and Chants* by Jackie Silberg and Pam Schiller.

Rhythm and Rhyme

As mentioned in the introduction, Block (2001) states that tapping to the rhythm of rhymes and poems develops temporal awareness, which creates awareness of and internalization of the rhythm of rhymes and poems.

To Have

A children's poem or nursery rhyme; rhythm sticks or instruments (optional)

To Do

- As you read a rhyme or poem to the children, suggest that they tap rhythm instruments or sticks or clap along to the beat of the rhyme or poem.
- Can the children hear and feel the rhythm of the rhyme or poem?

More to Do

- When the children have had ample experience clapping or tapping out the rhythm, ask them to use their whole bodies and to move around the room to the beat of the poem or rhyme.

It is best to choose a rhyme or poem with a fairly even rhythm throughout, and with at least a few stanzas so the children have time to get the feel of it. An excellent example is "Pawpaw Patch," which can be found in The *Complete Book of Rhymes, Songs, Poems, Fingerplays, and Chants* by Jackie Silberg and Pam Schiller.

Promotes phonological awareness

Where's the Sound?

This activity invites the children to listen for the sound of a specific letter and to say if it comes at the beginning, in the middle, or at the end of a word.

To Have

A list of words that include the same letter but in different places. A list of examples for the letter *s* follows:

- slither
- hassle
- pens
- castle
- names
- soap
- supper
- hurries
- bassoon
- books
- brings
- slink
- zebras

To Do

- Say the words very slowly at first.
- When the children hear the /s/ sound at the beginning of a word, they should point to or touch the top of their head (the "beginning" of the body).
- When they hear the /s/ sound in the middle of a word, they should point to or touch their tummy (the "middle" of the body).
- And when the /s/ sound appears at the end of the word, they should point to or touch their toes (the "end" of the body).

So Many Sounds

It is possible to make dozens of different sounds with a single sheet of paper by tearing, flicking, crumpling, smoothing, or folding it, among the myriad of possibilities. The children must listen carefully to each sound made with the paper in order to make one that hasn't been done before. This activity also promotes the development of problem-solving skills.

To Have

Sheet of paper

To Do

- Pass around a sheet of paper and invite each child to make a different sound with it.
- The children may not be ready to discover dozens of sounds, but you can assist by suggesting that they use a part of their body other than their hands. Possibilities include rubbing the paper on the head, blowing on it, smashing it underfoot, and rolling it up and using it as a horn.
- If the paper becomes unusable, replace it with another sheet of paper.

Ready, Set, Action!

Start slowly with this activity. Speak slowly and begin with only two commands at a time. When the children are ready, increase the challenge gradually.

To Have

No materials needed

To Do

- Give the children a short list of movements to do but ask them to wait until you have stopped speaking before they start doing them. Possible sequences include:

  - Jump twice; shake all over.
  - Clap twice; give yourself a hug.
  - Blink your eyes, bend over and straighten up.

- For three-part sequences, put some of the above together. For example: clap twice, blink your eyes, give yourself a hug.

Musical Memory

This activity tests children's auditory discrimination and memory. Start with just a few sounds so the children will be successful.

To Have

Instruments with distinctive sounds, such as a tambourine, a drum, a slide whistle, maracas, and bells

To Do

- Assign a particular movement to each of the instruments or sounds you have chosen and explain to the children that they should move that way when they hear the corresponding sound. For example, when you shake the tambourine, they should shake their bodies. When you bang the drum, they should stomp their feet. And when you play the slide whistle, they should move up and down in place.

- Mix up the order in which you play the instruments so the children will not know what to expect. (If possible, either turn your back to them so they will not see which instrument you pick up, or have them close their eyes.)

MARACAS   BELLS   HAND DRUM

More to Do

- For an added challenge, have the children recall sounds in sequence. Play three different sounds in a row. The children should remember the sequence of the sounds and display the corresponding actions in the correct order.

Musical Instruments from A to Z by Bobbie Kalman is both an introduction to numerous instruments and a review of the alphabet.

Play Me a Story

Isenberg and Jalongo (2002) recommend "musical storytelling"; they are the inspiration for this activity. These whimsical ideas will grab children's attention!

To Have

A story with which the children are familiar and whose words lend themselves to instrumentation (suggestion below); instruments appropriate for the story

To Do

- Read the story once through for the children.
- On the second reading, substitute instruments for words and phrases. Ask the children to tell you what was happening in the story when each instrument was played.
- On the final reading, ask the children to demonstrate what is happening as you play each instrument.

There are numerous illustrated versions of "Jack and the Beanstalk," which are perfect for musical storytelling. A slide whistle might represent Jack's climb up (ascent) and down (descent) the beanstalk; drums of different timbres might represent both Jack's and the giant's footsteps.

Which Word Doesn't Belong?

This activity requires children to listen for words that rhyme.

To Have

A list of words, most of which rhyme (for example, *cat, hat, sat, can, that, bat, pop, fat, mat, gnat, pat, sit, rat, spat, flat, thing, vat,* and *dog*)

To Do

- The children stand side by side along one side of the room. Stand on the opposite side of the room facing them.
- Every time you say a word that rhymes with the first word on your list (for example, cat), the children should take one small step forward.
- Every time you say a word that does not rhyme (such as dog), they should stand still.

More to Do

- Use this game for other groups of words. You might have older children take a step forward every time they hear a verb as opposed to a noun.

Play "The One That Doesn't Rhyme" from Hap Palmer's *Two Little Sounds: Fun with Phonics and Numbers* to reinforce this activity.

Jack Prelutsky has compiled more than 200 poems and rhymes in *Read-Aloud Rhymes for the Very Young.*

Develops auditory discrimination, phonological awareness, and word comprehension

What's in a Sound?

This game is similar to Listen Closely (page 25), but rather than focusing only on the beginning sound, it requires children to listen for long and short vowels. Discuss with the children the meanings of the words you plan to use.

To Have

Chart paper and markers

To Do

● On a piece of chart paper, write a few pairs of words that start with the same letters but have different meanings. Post the list where the children can see it.

● Read aloud a pair of words from the list.

● After you say each word, ask the children to do an action that describes or shows the word. If you say *peck*, they might demonstrate a pecking motion with their heads, imitating chickens. If you say *peek*, they might peek through their fingers, as though watching a scary movie. If you say the name of a body part, they might point to it or touch it.

● Other word combinations could include the following:

- tip/tie
- sit/sigh
- cheek/check
- top/toe
- huge/hug
- back/bake
- tail/tall
- steep/step

Silly Willy Discovers Fitness and Phonics, Volume 1: Short Vowels by Brenda Colgate integrates movement activities with short vowel phonics skills.

The Long and Short of It

This activity explores long and short vowels.

To Have

Chart paper (if posting the list) or regular paper

To Do

- For each vowel you explore with the children, make up a list of words using both the long and short versions of the vowel. For example, if you are exploring *i*, include words with long vowels, such as *silence, sigh, night, mighty, science, ride,* and *tidy,* and short vowels, such as *silk, trip, big, silver, sick, rim,* and *lift.*
- Have the children stand throughout the room.
- Every time they hear a word with a long vowel they make their bodies as long as possible and reach for the ceiling.
- Every time they hear a short vowel, they make their bodies short, squatting near the floor.
- At first, elongate the sound of the long *I* and shorten the sound of the short *I.* This will help the children learn to hear the difference. In the beginning saying a few words with long vowels and then a few words with short vowels will also help the children learn to hear the difference.
- As you call out the words on the list, mix up the long and short vowels.

  Note: If children respond incorrectly, simply move on. They will happily continue playing as long as no one makes them feel like failures! You only need to be concerned if a child continues to demonstrate a lack of understanding. You can then work with this child one-on-one at a later time.

LONG VOWEL

SHORT VOWEL

Silly Willy Discovers Fitness and Phonics, Volume 2: Long Vowels by Brenda Colgate integrates movement activities with long-vowel phonics skills.

Promotes awareness of rates of speech and auditory perception

Introducing Slow and Fast

*The concepts of slow and fast are only concepts to the children until they
physically experience them. These words are opposites and adjectives; they
involve the movement element of time and the musical element of tempo.
Identifying the tempo of a sound is part of auditory perception, awareness of
what we hear. By accompanying the children's movement with slow or fast
beats or music, they will have the opportunity to hear, feel, and see* slow *and*
fast! *These concepts are important because they are relevant to speech
patterns and to the rates at which we speak.*

To Have

Hand drum (optional)

To Do

- Talk with the children about *very slow* and *very fast*. Ask them to think about
  times when they might move either way.
- Beat on the drum or clap your hands very, very slowly. Ask the children to move
  in a way that the beats make them feel like moving.
- Repeat, beating on the drum with very fast beats.
- Continue, alternating between the two: *very slow* and *very fast*.

More to Do

- Play slow and fast music to make these concepts
  concrete.
- Give each child a chiffon scarf or ribbon stick and
  invite the children to demonstrate how slowly or
  quickly the prop can move with or without
  musical accompaniment.

Hap Palmer's *The Feel of Music* includes a song called "Slow and
Fast;" Bill Janiak's *Songs About Me* includes "The Slow Fast, Soft
Loud Clap Song." Rae Pica's *Moving & Learning Series* includes
"Moving Slow/Moving Fast" and "Marching Slow/Marching Fast."

CHAPTER 2

Speaking

According to Pinnell (1999), oral language is "…the foundation of literacy learning." Speaking aloud, singing, and chanting provide opportunities for children to experience and enjoy the sound of language and its rhythms, volumes, tempos, and textures in a variety of ways. With practice, children learn to enunciate clearly. As they are exposed to the rhythm of language and to physical expressions of that rhythm they are able to internalize the rhythm of words when they are reading.

The following activities expose children to rhythm, rhyme, syllables, phonemes, vowels, and more. They also give children a much-needed opportunity to express themselves!

SPLASH

HOP

TWIRL

Promotes enunciation, word comprehension, and awareness of rhyming

Twinkle, Twinkle, Little Star

Any time children sing, they are practicing enunciating or pronouncing words, some familiar and some not so familiar. Singing songs the children love broadens their vocabulary and acquaints them with literacy concepts such as rhyming.

To Have

No materials needed

To Do

- Discuss the meaning of the words *twinkle* and *diamond* and point out the rhyming words in the song (*star* and *are*, *high* and *sky*).
- Sing this longtime favorite with the children:

Twinkle, twinkle, little star,
How I wonder what you are!
Up above the world so high,
Like a diamond in the sky.
Twinkle, twinkle, little star,
How I wonder what you are!

- Ask the children to create actions to go with the lyrics.

This classic song appears on a number of recordings, including Hap Palmer's *Early Childhood Classics: Old Favorites with a New Twist* and *Early, Early Childhood Songs* by Ella Jenkins.

Read *Twinkle, Twinkle, Little Star* by Iza Trapani or *Twinkle, Twinkle, Little Star* by Jeanette Winter.

Old MacDonald

This old favorite gives children a chance to practice enunciating words, making animal sounds, and using the vowels e, i, and o.

To Have

No materials needed

To Do

- Sing the following song with the children:

  Old MacDonald had a farm, E-I-E-I-O
  And on that farm he had a [cow], E-I-E-I-O
  With a [moo-moo] here, and a [moo-moo] there
  Here a [moo], there a [moo],
  Everywhere a [moo-moo].
  Old MacDonald had a farm, E-I-E-I-O

- Substitute a new animal with a familiar sound with each succeeding verse.
- Stop after each verse and have the children act out the movements the animal might make as they make the appropriate sound. For example, a child might pretend to lick his "paws" as he meows.

More to Do

- Sing each verse separately or in a cumulative fashion. For example, the second verse might go like this:

  Old MacDonald had a farm, E-I-E-I-O
  And on that farm he had a pig, E-I-E-I-O
  With an oink-oink here, and an oink-oink there
  Here an oink, there an oink,
  Everywhere an oink, oink.
  With a moo-moo here, and a moo-moo there
  Here a moo, there a moo
  Everywhere a moo-moo.
  Old MacDonald had a farm, E-I-E-I-O!

Share a book version of the song such as *Old MacDonald Had a Farm* by Frances Cony.

Promotes enunciation and begins the process of decoding letters

B-I-N-G-O

It isn't until children can "decode" letters (understand that letters represent something) and spell that they can read and write successfully. This fun, familiar song can help children work toward that goal. Challenge them to say the letters as clearly as possible.

To Have

Chart paper or chalkboard (optional)

To Do

- Write the letters *B, I, N, G,* and *O* on a piece of chart paper or on the chalkboard.
- Sing the song with the children.

  There was a farmer had a dog,
  And Bingo was his name-o.
  B-I-N-G-O,
  B-I-N-G-O,
  B-I-N-G-O,
  And Bingo was his name-o.

- For the next round, substitute a clap (or a jump!) for the letter *B.* Continue, substituting one more clap for one more letter with each repeat, until all the letters have been replaced by claps.

More to Do

- Provide an early introduction to the vowels—although you do not even have to use that word—by substituting *A-E-I-O-U* for *B-I-N-G-O.*

Like Old MacDonald (page 45), this song is also available on Hap Palmer's *Early Childhood Favorites* and Bob McGrath's *Sing Along with Bob, Volume 2.*

Read Rosemary Wells' version of *Bingo.* She changed the dog's gender to female!

Naming Body Parts

Speech serves many functions for individuals. This game gives children the opportunity to identify and name familiar body parts.

To Have

No materials needed

To Do

- Say the following sentences and point to the appropriate body part(s). Have the children complete the sentences by calling out their answers.

  - I see with my _____.
  - I hear with my _____.
  - I smell with my _____.
  - I walk with my _____.
  - I talk with my _____.
  - I taste with my _____.
  - I touch with my _____.
  - I shrug with my _____.
  - I kiss with my _____.
  - I think with my _____.
  - I shampoo my _____.
  - I brush my _____.
  - I blink my _____.

More to Do

- Once children are successful at this activity, eliminate the pointing to make this a listening activity.

"The Body Poem" from Rae Pica and Richard Gardzina's CD, *Wiggle, Giggle, & Shake* offers an opportunity for children to listen and to identify body parts. Because each verse increases in speed, it is also an experience of tempo.

For an exploration of body parts we can see, as well as those we can't, read *Me and My Amazing Body* by Joan Sweeney.

Promotes pronunciation, word comprehension, and experience with rhythm and rhyming

The Eensy-Weensy Spider

Fingerplays are a wonderful tool for promoting literacy skills. They encourage children to speak or sing words out loud, and familiarize them with rhythm and rhyme. Adding actions to words makes them even more meaningful. And fingerplays are fun!

To Have

No materials needed

To Do

● With the children, sing the words to this popular fingerplay and act out the words.

The eensy-weensy spider went up the waterspout.
(creep your fingers upward)
Down came the rain and washed the spider out.
(show falling rain with your hands)
Out came the sun and dried up all the rain.
(use your arms to form shape of sun above your head)
And the eensy-weensy spider went up the spout again. (creep your fingers upward once more)

UP the WATERSPOUT

DOWN CAME the RAIN

More to Do

● Ask the children to demonstrate the following words with their whole bodies: *eensy-weensy, up, down, falling rain, sunshine,* and *spider.*

You'll find musical versions of this classic song on Hap Palmer's *Early Childhood Classics*; Bob McGrath's *Sing Along with Bob, Volume 1*; and Maryann "Mar" Harman's *Playing and Learning with Music.*

Children will love *The Eensy Weensy Spider* by Mary Ann Hoberman. It offers the familiar song as well as additional adventures for the spider!

Do-Re-Mi

The notes of the musical scale (do-re-mi-fa-so-la-ti-do) may seem to be about music only, but singing these notes helps children learn to enunciate as it also familiarizes them with vowels.

To Have

No materials needed

To Do

- Ask the children to echo what you sing as clearly as they can. Then sing each note of the scale, with the children echoing each note.

More to Do

- Once the children know the scale well and can sing it along with you, ask them to place their hands on their laps and to raise them a little higher with each note. Explain that their hands are *ascending* along with the notes.
- When the children have had a lot of practice with the scale, try it in reverse. Tell them that this is known as *descending*.
- When the children are familiar with long and short vowels, sing the scale slowly, asking them to make their bodies long on those notes with long vowels and to make their bodies short on those with short vowels. (It does not matter that *mi* is spelled m-i, as the children will not yet know that and will hear m-ē.)

Offers practice with rhythm and rhyme

Punchinello

Whether you and the children sing or chant this old favorite, it will let the children practice speaking rhythmically, hear rhyming words, and review what they learned.

To Have

No materials needed

To Do

- Form a circle with one child in the center. The children in the circle sing or chant:

  What can you do, Punchinello, funny fellow?
  What can you do, Punchinello, funny you?

- The child in the center demonstrates something learned that day or week (for example, the shape of a letter, the meaning of *narrow*, or how to hop). The children in the circle then sing or chant:

  We can do it, too, Punchinello, funny fellow.
  We can do it, too, Punchinello, funny you.

- Then they replicate Punchinello's action.
- If time permits, give every child a turn in the center. Otherwise, assign one or two Punchinellos per day.

THE LETTER "C"

More to Do

- Invite the children to think of words in addition to *fellow* that rhyme with Punchinello. Possibilities are *bellow, cello, hello, Jell-O, mellow,* and *yellow,* most of which you will have to suggest. After discussing the meaning of each word, invite the children to demonstrate the word with their bodies!

This Old Man

This familiar song offers children experience with rhythm, rhyme, repetition, and nonsense words. You may want to sing only one or two verses each time you do the activity. With enough repetition, the children will be able to sing the words.

To Have

One pair of rhythm sticks per child (optional)

To Do

- As you sing, the children clap (or tap, with rhythm sticks) the rhythm.
- When they hear the number in each verse, they hold up that many fingers.
- On the last line of each verse, they might roll their hands or rhythm sticks.

This old man, he played one;
He played knick-knack on his thumb.
With a knick-knack, paddy-whack
Give the dog a bone,
This old man came rolling home.

Additional verses:
This old man, he played two...he played knick-knack on his shoe...
...three...knee...
...four...door...
...five...hive...
...six...sticks...
...seven...pen...
...eight...gate...
...nine...rise and shine.
...ten...hen...

More to Do

- If the children are inspired, they can move their bodies to the song's rhythm.

Bob McGrath's *Songs and Games for Toddlers* includes "This Old Man" as a chant.

Two versions of *This Old Man* include one illustrated by Carol Jones and one illustrated by Pam Adams. Share them both and let the children compare and contrast the same story in the two books.

Little Miss Muffet

This traditional nursery rhyme is fun to say aloud and to act out. Talk to the children about such unfamiliar and old-fashioned words as tuffet, curds, and whey. (A tuffet is a low seat, like a stool. Curds and whey are the parts of milk used to make cheese, such as cottage cheese.)

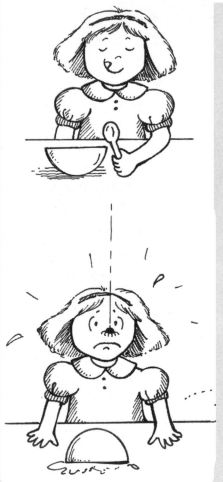

To Have

No materials needed

To Do

- Read the following nursery rhyme to the children.
- Then read each line individually and ask the children to repeat it and act it out simultaneously.

*Little Miss Muffet sat on a tuffet
Eating her curds and whey.
Along came a spider
And sat down beside her,
And frightened Miss Muffet away!*

Hap Palmer puts "Little Miss Muffet" to his original music on *Classic Nursery Rhymes*.

For a different take on the nursery rhyme, share the board book *Little Miss Muffet* by Tracey Campbell Pearson.

Mood Music

Music commonly conveys feelings, and since young children love to express their feelings, they are often the first to sense the mood of a song and respond to it. This is both a focused listening and a speaking activity because children are given the opportunity to listen and to express themselves.

To Have

A piece of music that conveys a specific mood (see below)

To Do

- Choose a piece of music that conveys a specific mood. For example, Bach's "Musette in D-Major," Beethoven's "Ode to Joy," Scott Joplin's "The Entertainer," and Bobby McFerrin's "Don't Worry, Be Happy" evoke happy feelings. Samuel Barber's "Adagio for Strings" and funeral marches convey sadness. An eerie piece of electronic music can evoke "scared," while "silly" might come to mind upon hearing "Baby Elephant Walk," "Syncopated Clock," or "Do Your Ears Hang Low?"
- Listen to one piece of music with the children.
- After listening for a while, ask some of the children to describe how the music made them feel.
- Continue with the same piece of music or with another selection. (With each repetition, be sure to call on different children.)

More to Do

- After the children have described how the music made them feel, invite them to show you. If they seem reluctant to do this, make it into a game of Statues by asking them to move while the music is playing and to freeze into statues when the music stops. Press the pause button. They won't be able to help moving in the way the music makes them feel!
- Repeat this activity often, using pieces that convey different moods. Also try using two opposite pieces during the same session. You might have the children move for a while to a happy piece and then switch to a sad piece. Go back and forth in this manner so they fully experience the contrast. You can use this as an opportunity to discuss the idea of opposites.

To inspire a discussion about moods, read *Today I Feel Silly: And Other Moods That Make My Day* by Jamie Lee Curtis. It follows a little girl through 13 different moods.

Introduces syllables and promotes the concept that words have rhythm

The Name Game

Children love this activity because they love to hear their own names!

To Have

No materials needed

To Do

- Sit in a circle with the children and clap the syllables of each child's first name while saying the name aloud. For example, Sa-man-tha would have three claps.
- After clapping each name, ask the group to mimic you.

More to Do

- Once the children are adept at clapping the syllables, add foot stamping. The children can do this most easily while still seated.

Read *Tikki Tikki Tembo* by Arlene Mosel and invite the children to clap the protagonist's longer-than-long name. The main characters in Steve Webb's *Tanka Tanka Skunk!* beat the cadence of words and names on their drums.

Echo

This exercise in the rhythm of syllables uses "Mary Had a Little Lamb," but you can do this activity with any popular nursery rhyme or poem that the children enjoy.

To Have

No materials needed

To Do

- Sit with the children in a circle and explain that they are going to echo what you say and mimic what you do.
- Recite the following nursery rhyme, breaking it into small pieces and clapping one clap per syllable as you say the words.

  Mary had a little lamb,
  Little lamb, little lamb.
  Mary had a little lamb,
  Its fleece was white as snow.

- Pause after each word or set of words so the children can repeat what you did. For example, clap twice as you say "Ma-ry" and invite the children to mimic you.
- Clap twice again as you say "had a," which the children repeat. Continue this pattern throughout the nursery rhyme.

The Book of Echo Songs compiled by John Feierabend consists of traditional echo songs for children that involve a leader singing a phrase and a group singing the phrase back.

Develops self-expression and communication skills

What I Did Last Summer

This activity gives children the opportunity to practice their language skills and make vital connections between cognitive, social/emotional, and physical domains. It validates and lends relevance to events in their lives.

To Have

No materials needed

To Do

- Choose a category to discuss with the children: what they did over the weekend, their favorite animal, what they would like to get for a birthday present. Or let them choose their own topics.
- Ask one child to respond to a question on the topic and to demonstrate his response with movement. For example, if a child says that his favorite animal is a cat, he would then move like a cat. If he tells you he went on a picnic over the weekend, he would act out that activity.
- Ask the rest of the children to imitate that child's movement.
- Repeat the process, giving each child a turn to answer and to demonstrate his response.

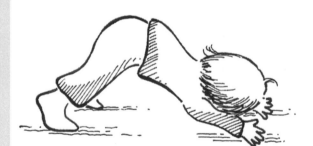

CAT STRETCHING

A Time for Rhyme

Children love rhyming words. This multi-sensory activity offers the opportunity to hear, say, and act out the rhyming words you choose to explore.

To Have

List of rhyming words (a rhyming dictionary saves valuable time preparing activities like this); chart paper and markers

To Do

- Make up a list of rhyming words in advance and post the words for the children to see.
- Say a word on your list, for example, *bat.* Ask the children to repeat the word and to perform an action that might depict the word. Some might pretend to swing a bat; others might flap their wings like the other kind of bat.
- Continue this process with other words that rhyme with the first word you have used, such as *cat, fat, hat, mat, pat, rat,* and *sat.*

A BAT

SWINGING A BAT

Among Hap Palmer's songs about rhymes are "Rhyme Time Band" on *Can Cockatoos Count by Twos?* and "The One That Doesn't Rhyme" on *Two Little Sounds: Fun with Phonics and Numbers.*

Offers practice with self-expression, oral language, and love of language

A Voice for Every Occasion

Children love to explore different ways to use their voices. This activity explores four ways: whispering, speaking, shouting, and singing.

To Have

No materials needed

To Do

- Ask the group as a whole to say their names out loud.
- Then as a group ask them to whisper their names and then shout their names.
- Finally, challenge them to sing their names!

More to Do

- Say, whisper, shout, and sing the words of a nursery rhyme or poem.
- Tell the children that for this activity, walking is the movement that goes along with the speaking voice. Brainstorm with them on movements that might go with each of the other voices. For example, they might determine that tiptoeing goes with whispering, stomping goes with shouting, and dancing goes with singing. Next, call out one of the types of voice and challenge the children to say their names in that voice while doing the corresponding movement.
- Once the children are familiar with this activity, invite them, one at a time, to demonstrate one of the predetermined movements without any sound accompanying it. The rest of the children then guess which voice is being represented.

Show and Tell

This classic activity uses children's innate desire to "show and tell" to practice speaking before a group—what adults call public speaking!

To Have

Items from each child's home

To Do

- The children take turns showing what they have brought from home and explaining its significance to them.

A BALL   A DOLL   A YO YO

More to Do

- After each child has had a turn, invite one at a time to demonstrate something brought in that day, either through movement or by taking on its shape. A child might make a round shape with his body to illustrate a ball someone brought in. The rest of the children guess which item is being demonstrated!

Read *Show and Tell* by Robert N. Munsch or *The King of Show-and-Tell* by Abby Klein.

The Feely Box

Children reach into a box and identify its contents without looking. This is an age-old early childhood activity. This version of the activity lets children express themselves with both verbal and body language. It also encourages them to use adjectives, too.

To Have

A box containing items of many different textures, such as a feather, a stuffed animal, a piece of burlap, a piece of silk or satin, and a rock

To Do

- Give each child a turn to reach into the box, pick an item, and guess what it is. After he has guessed, the child says how the item made him feel. (For example, the piece of burlap might make him feel "scratchy.")
- The child then demonstrates with his whole body how the item made him feel. He might, for example, scratch his arms.

It's in the Bag

This activity offers children an element of surprise, which they love, and an opportunity to describe the items that surprise them.

To Have

A large bag or sack; a variety of familiar objects (The number of objects should equal or exceed the number of children playing. Possibilities include a plastic shovel, a whisk broom, a maraca, a tambourine, a pencil, a ruler, and a rubber ball.)

To Do

- Each child takes a turn reaching into the bag and pulling out an object. The child describes what the object is and how it is used or what it feels like.
- The rest of the children demonstrate through movement how the object is used or how it feels.

Body Sounds

*This word comprehension activity teaches children about verbs that describe
things the body does and nouns that describe sounds the body makes! Mostly,
it is about having fun with words.*

To Have

No materials needed

To Do

- Talk to the children about
  the sounds of a cough,
  sneeze, yawn, hiccup, giggle,
  and snore.
- Then say the words, one at
  a time, and invite the
  children to demonstrate
  how their body moves when
  they act out the selected
  word.

Read *"Stand Back," Said the Elephant, "I'm Going to Sneeze!"* by Patricia Thomas,
The Flea's Sneeze by Lynn Downey or, for a more scientific approach, *Why I Sneeze,
Shiver, Hiccup, and Yawn* by Melvin Berger.

Slow and Fast Imagery

This activity uses imagery to explore the concept of tempo. This inspires the children to use their imaginations.

To Have

No materials needed

To Do

● Discuss the creatures and objects listed below to ensure that the children are familiar with them. Ask them to tell you how they think the pairs of creatures or objects differ from one another. They may say, for example, that a turtle is green and a squirrel is gray. That's okay; if they don't mention the speed at which these creatures and objects move, you can introduce the subject.

● Ask the children to move like the following, contrasting the two suggested extremes:

  • a turtle/a squirrel racing across the lawn
  • a race car/a very big truck
  • a hummingbird/an eagle soaring
  • a snake slithering through the grass/a snail

Read a version of the Aesop fable, "The Tortoise and the Hare," as an introduction or follow-up to this activity.

Promotes awareness of sound

Introducing Soft and Loud

Like slow *and* fast *(see Introducing Slow and Fast on page 41 and Slow and Fast Imagery on page 63), the concepts* soft *and* loud *teach a variety of lessons. They are opposites and adjectives. They also relate to the musical element of volume, which is relevant to tone of voice.*

To Have

Hand drum (optional)

To Do

- Discuss *very soft* and *very loud* with the children. Ask them to identify some times when they might speak softly or loudly. When do they move loudly or softly? For example, they might move loudly when they are mad and stomping their feet; they might move softly when trying to be quiet and tiptoeing. Ask questions to encourage them to talk. "Which do you like better, speaking softly or loudly?" "Would you rather move softly or loudly? Why?"
- Alternate between very soft and very loud drumbeats (or hand claps). Ask the children to move in ways the sounds inspire them to move.

More to Do

- Play soft music and invite the children to tiptoe, move like a cat sneaking up on a bird, or float. Then play loud music and suggest that they stamp their feet, swing their arms forcefully, or move heavily like a dinosaur or elephant.
- Give the children maracas or shakers and invite them to show you how softly or loudly the prop can move, with or without a musical accompaniment.

Children's songs that offer a contrast between soft and loud volumes include "Soft and Loud" from Hap Palmer's *The Feel of Music;* "Play Soft, Play Loud" from Jill Gallina's *Rockin' Rhythm Band;* and "Moving Softly/Moving Loudly" from Rae Pica's *Moving & Learning Series.*

Buzz and Ollie's Loud, Soft Adventure by Donna Sloan Thorne is a wonderful accompaniment to these activities.

Just Like It Sounds

The term used to describe words that sound like what they mean is onomatopoeia. You do not have to use this term with the children, but you can give them a chance to experience saying and expressing fun words that help develop a love of language.

To Have

Large cards or chart paper and markers

To Do

● Write the following onomatopoeiac words on large cards or chart paper.

● Present the words one at a time. Many other words can go on your list, too!

● The children *say* the word as they do the action. They can each move in the way each feels best expresses the word.

- boom
- plop
- wobble
- gobble
- swish
- whoops
- quack
- splash
- hop
- drip
- toot
- twirl
- squeak
- bang

Bang! Bang! Toot Toot; Snap! Snap! Buzz Buzz; and *Brrrm! Whoosh,* all by Rich Cowley, are wonderful accompaniments to this activity.

Introduces alliteration

Echo II

The term alliteration *describes a string of words that have the same beginning sound. Many familiar tongue twisters use alliteration, which is what helps "twist the tongue!"*

To Have

No materials needed

To Do

- Slowly clap out and speak the syllables of one or more of the following tongue twisters, combining them in groups of two or three.
- Have the children echo you after each grouping. (Two-syllable words are hyphenated below for simplicity.)
- Stop or slow down if the children become frustrated. The point of tongue twisters is to have fun!

- Inch-worms inch-ing
- The myth of Miss Muf-fet
- Love-ly le-mon lin-a-ment
- A big black bug bit a big black bear.
- She sells sea-shells down by the sea-shore.
- Pe-ter Pi-per picked a peck of pic-kled pep-pers.
- How much wood would a wood-chuck chuck if a wood-chuck could chuck wood?
- Friend-ly Frank flips fine flap-jacks.

Have fun with *Busy Buzzing Bumblebees and Other Tongue Twisters,* collected by Alvin Schwartz.

CHAPTER 3

Reading

This chapter is more about pre-reading than reading itself. Before children are ready to read, they must master the mystery of language. Many of the activities in the previous two chapters help children do that; the activities in this chapter advance the process.

Reading is about recognizing and decoding letters, early spelling, and word comprehension. The following activities promote all of these areas while also introducing and reinforcing such parts of speech as prepositions, nouns, verbs, adjectives, adverbs, and opposites.

The activities begin with *directionality* (top-to-bottom and left-to-right progression of print) followed by *cross-lateral* experiences. Hannaford (1995) explains that reading demands cross-lateral eye-hand coordination. Practicing cross-lateral movements (moving the left arm and the right leg simultaneously, and vice versa) helps promote eye-hand coordination. It requires crossing the vertical midline of the body (the invisible line running down the center of the body, from head to toe). Cross-lateral patterns require the left and right hemispheres of the brain to communicate across the corpus callosum, which is essential to reading and writing skills. Corso (1993) discovered that many children who are unable to cross the midline read and write down the vertical center of the page!

Hannaford (1995) asserts that the most "natural" way for children to learn to read is "through image, emotion, and spontaneous movement."

SLITHERING
SNAKE

Promotes directionality, which is necessary for reading

Top to Bottom

Reading (and writing) involves going from the top to the bottom of a page. This activity provides practice with the experience of moving in a downward direction. The more children physically experience directionality, the more it is imprinted on their bodies and in their minds. This means that the more comfortable children are with moving their bodies in a downward direction, the more comfortable they will be moving their eyes in that direction.

To Have

No materials needed

To Do

- The children move the following from up high to down low.

  - one (then the other) hand
  - both hands together
  - the nose
  - a shoulder
  - their belly button
  - their whole body (Pop up and do it again!)

More to Do

- For a greater challenge, combine top-to-bottom spatial orientation with word comprehension by asking children to show you the differences among these words by moving from high to low positions:

  - shrink
  - melt
  - collapse
  - shrivel

"High & Low" from Rae Pica's *Moving & Learning Series* reinforces spatial orientation.

The Grand Old Duke of York

This song has long been a favorite of children. When children act it out they experience rhythm while also reinforcing the concepts of up *and* down.

To Have

No materials needed

To Do

- The more children experience directionality physically, the more it is imprinted on their bodies and in their minds. The more comfortable children are with moving their bodies in a downward direction, the more comfortable they will be moving their eyes in that direction.
- Sing the song below to the children, then sing it again slowly as the children act it out.

The grand old Duke of York,
He had ten thousand men.
He marched them up the hill;
He marched them down again.

And when you're up, you're up.
And when you're down, you're down.
And when you're halfway in between,
You're neither up nor down.

The Grand Old Duke of York by Maureen Roffey adds fun new verses and to the original nursery rhyme!

Promotes directionality and laterality

Left to Right

Practicing left-to-right movements is excellent preparation for reading (and writing). Moving from one side of the body to the other gives children an opportunity to cross the midline.

To Have

No materials needed

To Do

- Have the children stand side-by-side in lines, facing the same direction.
- Designate objects or places in the room to indicate their left and right sides. For example, the windows are on their left side and the door is on the right.
- Moving always from left to right (for example, from the windows to the door), invite the children to perform the following activities and any others you can think of (demonstrating at first, if necessary).

  - Turn their heads.
  - Draw a line on the floor with their big toes.
  - Move both arms. Do this at various levels in space: at shoulder height, above the head, and below the waist.
  - Move one arm at a time.
  - Take several steps to the side.
  - Jump, hop, or slide.

More to Do

- Challenge the children to perform group activities that involve moving left to right. For example, they can hold hands and circle to the right; hold hands in a line and slide to the left and then to the right; or they might do The Wave, moving from left to right.
- When the children have begun to learn left from right, incorporate these words into the activity.
- Have the children move their arms left to right, starting with their arms overhead and working their way down to the floor. Or they can turn their heads left to right while they move their bodies lower and lower toward the floor.

Hap Palmer's *Getting to Know Myself* includes a song called "Left and Right."

Read Mavis Smith's *Which Way, Ben Bunny?: A Lift-the-Flap Book About Left and Right.*

This Is My Friend

This cooperative activity, adapted from Orlick (1978), offers children a chance to experience movement that goes from left to right, as well as concepts of sequencing (in this case, a series of movements one following one the other) and low and high.

To Have

No materials needed

To Do

- Stand in a circle with the children with everyone holding hands.
- Raise the hand of the child to your right (so the movement goes left to right) and say, "This is my friend _____."
- That child says her name and raises the arm of the next child in the circle and says, "This is my friend _____."
- The process continues all the way around the circle until every child has had a chance to say his name and all arms are in the air.
- The group then takes a big bow.

More to Do

- Once the children know one another's names, they can introduce each other instead of themselves. For example, Kara might raise the arm of the child to her right and say, "This is my friend, Tony."

My Friends by Taro Gomi is one of many children's books that explore the concept of friendship. Use it to initiate a discussion about friends. It has a lot of movement in it, which makes it great for reenacting.

Which Way Do We Go?

This activity provides additional practice with the spatial directions of up, down, left, and right.

To Have

A large card with a large arrow drawn on it

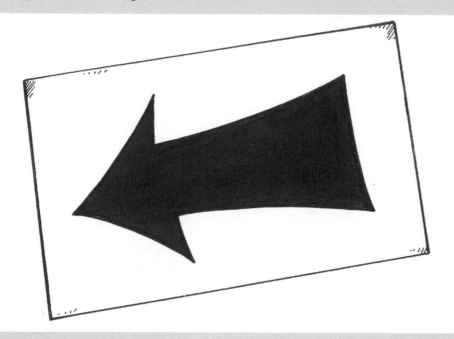

To Do

- Display the card with the arrow pointed in one of four directions.
- If it is pointed upward, the children stretch toward the ceiling. If it is pointed downward, the children crouch down. If it is pointed left or right, the children take a step in that direction.

For a fun exploration of *up* and *down*, read *Up, Up, Down!* by Robert N. Munsch.

Cross-Lateral Creatures

The children may feel too mature to practice crawling on their tummies and creeping on their hands and knees, but they'll still find it fun to pretend to be a variety of critters. And pretending to be critters offers great cross-lateral experience!

To Have

No materials needed

To Do

- Invite the children to move like the following creatures:

  - dogs
  - snakes
  - spiders
  - rabbits
  - eels
  - cats
  - birds
  - turtles
  - lizards

SLITHERING SNAKE

More to Do

- Play Ducks, Cows, Cats, and Dogs (page 31 in Chapter 1: Listening). Children can never have too much cross-lateral experience!

Diane L. Burns has created two field guides appropriate for this activity: *My Take-Along Guide of Snakes, Salamanders and Lizards* and *My Take-Along Guide of Frogs, Toads and Turtles.*

Offers practice crossing the body's midline

Cross-Crawl

For a quick "brain break" that involves cross-lateral movement, use this activity adapted from Brain Gym *(Dennison & Dennison, 1989).*

To Have

No materials needed

To Do

- Stand with your back to the children and ask them to imitate you.
- Slowly and repeatedly alternate touching your left elbow to your raised right knee and your right elbow to your raised left knee. (If the children have trouble bringing their elbows to their knees, they can touch one knee with the opposite hand.)
- If the children have difficulty imitating your movements, turn around and face them, creating a mirror image for them that they can imitate.

Do As I Do

This activity is similar to the Mirror Game (page 99), but all the activities involve crossing the midline.

To Have

No materials needed

To Do

● Stand facing the children and ask them to imitate your movements. Then do actions such as the following:

- Pat the left shoulder with the right hand and vice-versa.
- Reach with one arm across the body.
- Cross and then uncross one ankle over the other ankle.
- Place the left hand on the right side and vice-versa.
- Make an X shape with the forearms. Uncross and repeat.
- Wrap one arm at a time around the waist, resulting in a hug.

ONE ANKLE OVER the OTHER

"X" SHAPE

WRAP ONE ARM AROUND WAIST

Promotes word comprehension and a love of reading

Once Upon a Time

Reading specialists and early childhood professionals have long known that reading to children inspires enthusiasm for reading. When children also have the opportunity to act out stories, their level of enthusiasm soars, their recall of the order of events improves, and their word comprehension expands.

To Have

A book, story, or nursery rhyme with a strong plot and characters (see below)

To Do

- Choose a book, story, or nursery rhyme to read to the children. Read the book once through.
- Then read it again much slower the second time, and invite the children to act it out. Books that lend themselves to dramatization include *Caps for Sale* by Esphyr Slobodkina, *The Napping House* by Audrey Wood, and *Stellaluna* by Janell Cannon. Other good choices include such classic tales as "Jack and the Beanstalk," "Henny Penny," "Hansel and Gretel," "The Three Billy Goats Gruff," and "Goldilocks and the Three Bears." For something quick, choose a nursery rhyme such as "Jack Be Nimble," "Jack and Jill," or "Humpty Dumpty."

Five Little Monkeys Jumping on the Bed by Eileen Christelow is perfect for this activity. The book also encourages jumping, a locomotor skill with cardiovascular, strength, and endurance benefits. Assign one child to be the mother, one to be the doctor, and the rest to be the monkeys.

All About the Alphabet

This exercise in letter recognition helps children differentiate between the straight and curving lines that comprise the letters of the alphabet. It promotes the ability to replicate physically what the eyes see, a skill children need for writing.

To Have

Chart paper and markers

To Do

- Write the letters of the alphabet (lowercase, uppercase, or both) on a piece of chart paper.
- Point out to the children that some letters have straight lines, some have curvy lines, and some have both.
- Then point to a letter (those with the fewest lines such as *I, T, C, L, O, V,* and *X* are the easiest to reproduce) and ask the children to make that letter with their bodies or body parts. Repeat with several letters.

More to Do

- Sing the chorus of the song, "YMCA" by the Village People slowly and invite the children to depict these four letters.

- When the children are ready for more challenging letters such as *B, G, K, R,* and *P* and for the greater challenge of working cooperatively, ask them to create letters in pairs and trios.

Read Audrey Wood's *Alphabet Adventure* and *Alphabet Mystery*; both will get children excited about letters.

Develops letter recognition

All About the Alphabet II

Children's knowledge of letters has been "found to be the single best predictor of first-year reading achievement." (Machado 2003, p. 520).

To Have

Large cutout letters

To Do

- Scatter large cutout letters on the floor. Challenge the children to:

  - Kneel on top of a letter that has only straight lines.
  - Sit next to a letter that has only curving lines.
  - Stand behind a letter that has both straight and curving lines.

- These are a few things children can do. You may want to present more challenges.

More to Do

- The children move to a letter found in their names or that starts their names.

Play selections from Brenda Colgate's *Silly Willy Moves Through the ABCs*. The song, "Bend It, Twist It, Turn It" from her *Silly Willy's Pre-Jump Rope Skills* asks children to create letters with rope.

Chicka Chicka Boom Boom by Bill Martin, Jr. and John Archambault is a fun alphabet book.

All About the Alphabet III

This simple activity expands the ideas of the previous two activities (All About the Alphabet and All About the Alphabet II), while helping children understand that letters represent sounds.

To Have

Large blank index cards and markers

To Do

- Print each letter of the alphabet on a large index card. Hold up a card and say the letter, followed by the sound it makes.
- The children then move to, point to, or touch something in the room that begins with that letter.
- For example, hold up the letter *d* card, say "d," and then make the /d/ sound. The children might move to or point to a desk, the door, or a drawer.

More to Do

- When the children are ready, use several cards to display letter combinations. For example, if you hold up a card with *ch*, the children might move or point to a chair, the chalkboard, or a piece of chalk.

The CD/cassette/book combo called *ABC Songs: Alphabet Sounds* (Kidzup Productions) teaches young children the sounds of each letter of the alphabet.

Offers practice in spatial awareness and understanding of prepositions

Over and Under

Prepositions are little words with great significance for language. This activity helps children understand two prepositions; the children will think they are playing a simple game with a ball!

To Have

A playground or small beach ball

To Do

- Stand in a circle with the children with each child facing another child's back.
- Pass the ball backward *over* your head to the child behind you. That child does the same, and the ball goes all the way around the circle in this manner.
- Then ask everyone to stand with their legs apart and pass the ball *under* their bodies to the person behind them.
- When the children are comfortable with both ways of passing the ball, invite them to do it in alternation: one child passes it over her head and the next child passes it under his body.
- Be sure to use the words *over* and *under* in connection with what the children are doing.

OVER   UNDER

Over and *under* are just two of the opposites explored in *Over Under* by Marthe Jocelyn.

Over, Under, and More

This activity increases the understanding of positional words (prepositions) through physical experience of the concepts. You do not even need to use the word *prepositions!*

To Have

Materials for an obstacle course (cardboard boxes, jump ropes, plastic hoops, classroom furniture, and so on); display cards with illustrated and written directions

To Do

- Set up a simple obstacle course that includes at each point a card with a direction (both drawn and written) indicating which way the children should move: *over, under, around,* or *through.*
- Talk with the children about the positional words that they are going to experience when doing the obstacle course, and explain the cards to them.
- Then lead them through the course, explaining what you are doing. For example, you might say, "Now we are going *under* the rope. Next we'll go *through* the box."

More to Do

- Once the children are familiar with the course, make slight changes to it. For example, if the children were previously expected to go *under* a rope suspended between two pieces of furniture, lay the rope flat and direct them to step *over* it.
- Place any object on the floor and invite the children to discover how many different ways they can move *over* or *around* it.
- If you have a low balance beam, challenge the children to find two or more ways to move *over* it, such as stepping, jumping, or slithering over it. How many ways can they find to move across it? Possibilities include scooting on their bottoms, sliding on their tummies, walking, tiptoeing, or stepping sideways.

To reinforce these concepts, sing and then discuss such songs as "Ring Around the Rosie," "The Bear Went Over the Mountain," "She'll Be Comin' 'Round the Mountain," and "Over the River and Through the Woods."

Share *Over, Under, and Through* by Tana Hoban with the children.

Reinforces understanding of positional prepositions

Take Your Positions

This word comprehension activity reinforces more challenging positional prepositions.

To Have

One jump rope per child

To Do

● Each child places her rope on the floor and does the following:

* Stands *beside* the rope.
* Stands with the rope *behind* her.
* Stands with the rope *in front* of her.
* Stands *near* the rope.
* Stands *far* from the rope.
* Walks *around* the rope.
* Walks *toward* her rope and then continues walking past it.
* Walks *toward* her rope again.
* Stands with the rope *between* her feet.
* Stands *on top* of her rope.
* Stands *by* her rope.
* Lies *across* her rope.
* Stands with the rope *in* her hands.
* Holds the rope *against* her body.

Silly Willy's Pre-Jump Rope Skills by Brenda Colgate offers children a variety of activities with ropes.

Read *Under, Over, by the Clover: What Is a Preposition?* by Brian P. Cleary or *Behind the Mask: A Book About Prepositions* by Ruth Heller.

The Alphabet in Action

This activity offers multiple benefits. You can use it over weeks or months. When children see words that begin with the same letter, they make progress toward decoding letters. When they see the words, hear them used in a sentence, and then act them out, they advance toward word recognition and comprehension. Because some of the words are nouns and some are verbs, they will begin to understand the distinction between these two parts of grammar.

To Have

Large index cards or poster board and markers

To Do

- Write words that start with the same letter on separate cards or in very large letters on a poster board.
- Hold up a card with a word on it or point to the word on the poster. Say the word, discuss its meaning, and then use it in a simple sentence.
- Note: The list includes simple words, such as dog, eye, and eat, and more complex words, such as absorb, meditate, and ukulele. Select words that are suitable for the skills and abilities of the children in your class.
- Have the children show you with their bodies what the word makes them think of.
- You can choose nouns or verbs from the list below, or you can alternate between the two, explaining that one kind of word represents a person or thing and the other represents an action. (Note: The children may show you an action to represent a noun, but that does not mean they have failed to understand. For example, a likely response to the word *carpenter* would be a hammering action. Where appropriate, I have included the same word in both categories. For instance, *lap* as a noun means something you can sit on. As a verb, it is the way a cat drinks milk.)

Following is a list of words to choose from:

A

Nouns: ache, air, angel, ankle, ant, ape, apple, arm, ax
Verbs: absorb, agree, aim, arch, argue, ate

B

Nouns: back, banana, bark, baseball, bear, beast, belly, bird, bottom, branch, bread, breeze, bumblebee, bump

Verbs: bake, bang, bark, bend, bite, blink, bounce, bow, break, breathe, brush, burst

C

Nouns: cake, candle, cap, cape, car, cat, cereal, chair, cheek, chest, chimp, chin, claw, clothes, cloud, computer, curve

Verbs: catch, cheer, chew, chirp, chop, clap, clean, cling, comb, crawl, creep, crunch

D

Nouns: desert, desk, dessert, dimple, dog, door, duck

Verbs: dance, dash, devour, dive, dodge, drag, draw, dress, dribble, drill, drop

E

Nouns: ear, earth, eel, elbow, envelope, eye, eyebrow

Verbs: eat, elevate, exhale, explode, explore

F

Nouns: face, fear, feet, finger, flag, flake, flame, floor, flower, food, football, footstep, forehead, fork, friend, frog

Verbs: fade, faint, fall, feel, fill, flail, flap, flee, flinch, fling, flit, flow, flutter, fly, focus, freeze, frown

G

Nouns: gap, ghost, glee, goat, goo, grape, grass, group

Verbs: gallop, giggle, give, glide, glow, golf, grasp, glare, grin, groan, grow, growl, grunt

H

Nouns: hair, hand, head, heart, heel, height, hem, hen, hip, hole

Verbs: hail, haul, hear, hide, hold, hop, howl, hug, hum

I

Nouns: I, ice, iceberg, ice cream, idea, illness, inch, indoors, insect, island, itch

Verbs: ignite, ignore, illustrate, imagine, inflate, inhale, inspect, invite

J

Nouns: jaw, jazz, jet, jitters, joint, joy

Verbs: jabber, jiggle, jog, jot, jump

K

Nouns: kayak, ketchup, kindness, king, kitchen, kite, knee, knife, knight
Verbs: kick, kiss, knit, knead, kneel, knock

L

Nouns: ladder, lake, lamb, lamp, land, lap, lawn, leg, letter, line, lips, lightbulb
Verbs: land, lap, lean, leap, lie, lift, look, lower, lunge

M

Nouns: mare, marionette, mitten, monkey, moon, moose, mound, mouse, mouth, muscle
Verbs: mash, meditate, melt, mend, mow, move, mop, mope

N

Nouns: nail, nap, neck, nest, night, noise, nose, nothing
Verbs: nail, neigh, nibble, nod, nudge

O

Nouns: oar, oatmeal, ocean, octopus, odor, oil, ointment, onion, orange, orangutan, organist, outdoors
Verbs: observe, ogle, ooze, open, operate, orbit, overflow

P

Nouns: pain, pan, paper clip, pea, peace, peach, peak, pear, peel, pencil, pep, person, pie, plum, pole, pool, present
Verbs: pace, paddle, paint, pant, park, pat, pay, peck, peek, peep, perch, pinch, pitch, pluck, point, pose, pounce, pound, pour, pout, print, pucker, pull, push

Q

Nouns: quarter, queen, quickness
Verbs: quack, quake, quarrel, quiver

R

Nouns: rabbit, rain, rainbow, roof, room, rose, roundness, rowboat, royalty, ruler
Verbs: race, rake, reach, read, ride, rip, rise, roar, rock, roll, row, run, rush

S

Nouns: sailboat, salt, seaweed, shin, shoulder, snake, soccer, socks, soil, sound, spider, spoon, squirrel, star, sun, sweater
Verbs: saw, sing, sink, sip, sit, skip, slither, smile, soar, soothe, spin, stalk, step, sway, swim, swing

T

Nouns: table, tail, teapot, tear, telephone, tennis, thigh, thirst, thumb, time, toe, tongue, top, tooth, tree, truck, tummy
Verbs: talk, tap, tear, teeter, tilt, tiptoe, topple, tremble, tumble, turn, twist

U

Nouns: ukulele, umbrella, unicorn, universe, U-turn
Verbs: underline, undress, undulate, unfold, unite

V

Nouns: Valentine, vapor, vase, vegetable, veil, velvet, vine, volcano
Verbs: vacuum, vibrate, view, visit, vroom

W

Nouns: wagon, waist, wall, wasp, water, wave, web, wind, windshield wipers, winter, witch, wrist
Verbs: waddle, wade, wait, walk, wash, wave, weep, whisper, wiggle, wink

X

Nouns: xylophone, x-ray
Verbs: x-ray

Y

Nouns: yacht, yam, yardstick, yarn, yellow jacket, yolk
Verbs: yank, yap, yawn, yell

Z

Nouns: zebra, zest, zoo
Verbs: zap, zigzag, zip, zoom

Everything to Spend the Night from A to Z by Ann Whitford Paul is great fun and offers a collection of nouns and verbs.

Find the Letter

This activity imprints the letters of the alphabet on the children's minds and bodies.

To Have

Large, cutout letters, several of each

To Do

- Scatter large cutout letters around the floor.
- Challenge the children to find different letters. For example, they might look for the first letter in their name.
- When they find the letter, ask them to take on the shape of the letter with their whole body or body parts.
- Ask them to find the first letter of a specific word; for example, *cat*. When they find it, ask them to take on the shape of the letter *c*.
- Continue this process with letters and words that are familiar to the children.

Ted   Frannie

More to Do

- When the children are familiar with a number of words, write each word on a large card (several cards should show the same word) and scatter them around the floor. When the children find the word you have designated, ask them to demonstrate something the word brings to mind, rather than the shape of the letters. For example, if they find the word *dog*, they might bark or move like a dog on all fours.

Accompany this activity with Jean Marzollo's *I Spy Little Letters*.

Promotes word recognition and print awareness

Color Me...

This simple activity promotes word and color recognition.

To Have

Large cards; markers, crayons, or paint in a variety of colors

To Do

- Print the words for various colors on separate large cards using the same color of marker, crayon, or paint for the corresponding word. For example, write the word "blue" with a blue marker or crayon.
- Hold up one of the cards and say the name of the color written on it. The children then point to, move to, or touch something in the room in that color.
- Repeat with each of the color cards.

More to Do

- When the children have had ample experience, play the game without saying the name of the color on the card you are holding up.

Follow up with songs on Kimbo's *Songs About Colors and Shapes.*

Brown Bear, Brown Bear, What Do You See? by Bill Martin, Jr. is a wonderful accompaniment to this exploration of color.

Words in Action

Words have much greater relevance to children when they act out the meaning of the word than if they simply hear or read the word. This word comprehension activity is specifically about action words, or verbs.

To Have

Chart paper and markers

To Do

- Choose action words (verbs) from the following list:
  - Traveling words include: waddle, sneak, pounce, float, bounce, slither, and stalk
  - Non-traveling action words include: melt, shake, collapse, shrink, wriggle, spin, shiver, and tremble
  - Verbs that pause the action include: freeze, pause, flop, drop, and stop
- Write a few words on chart paper and post the list for the children to see. Engage the children in a discussion about the meaning of the words with the children.
- Call out one word at a time, and have the children demonstrate the word's meaning.

More to Do

- When the children are ready, step up the challenge by presenting two or more words at a time to act out in sequence. For example, you might invite them to "stamp and shake." Later, you might lengthen that to "stamp, stop, and shake."
- The next challenge is for the children to demonstrate the words you give them in any order they like, performing as many repetitions of each as they choose.
- Choose a story with plenty of action words. After reading it aloud, choose an appropriate section and ask the children to act it out.
- For children who can read, place action word cards face down on the floor. At your signal, have them run to any card, turn it over, and act out the word. Have them run to a different card when you give the next signal.

Barnyard Dance! by Sandra Boynton includes such action words as *stomp, clap, bow, twirl, spin, prance, swing,* and *trot. Dinosaurumpus!* by Tony Mitton uses *romp, shudder,* and *shake* in repeating stanzas.

Promotes word comprehension and understanding of opposites

All About Opposites

Children are more likely to grasp the meaning of opposites by exploring opposites with their bodies! This activity gives them that chance.

To Have

Chart paper and marker

To Do

- Ask the children to demonstrate the following words with their bodies or body parts. Feel free to add other words to the list.
- Write the words on chart paper and post the list for children to see: up/down; small/large; long/short; forward/backward; happy/sad; high/low; front/back; tiny/enormous; wide/narrow; top/bottom.

More to Do

- Play Charades! The children take turns acting out one of the above words, with the other children guessing the word.
- Children work in pairs to demonstrate the opposites, with each partner demonstrating one pair. If you call out "high," for example, one partner forms a high shape, such as standing on tiptoe with arms above the head. As that partner holds her position, call out "low," which her partner demonstrates (for example, crouching near the floor). In this way, it is possible for the children to *see* the contrast.
- For a greater challenge, do not reveal the opposite of the word given. For example, if you call out "*forward,*" one child should act out the word and her partner should act out the opposite, without being told the word "*backward.*" Call out another word, which the partner demonstrates. The other partner then demonstrates its opposite.

FACING
FORWARD

FACING
BACKWARD

Songs dedicated to opposites are challenging but fun. Among them are "Opposites" on Greg and Steve's *Fun and Games* and "Say the Opposite" on Hap Palmer's *Can a Cherry Pie Wave Goodbye?*

Opposites by Sandra Boynton reinforces the concept of opposites as does *Elephant, Elephant: A Book of Opposites* by Francesco Pittau.

Light and Heavy Words in Action

This activity uses verbs that indicate light and heavy movements. Verbs for light movements include sway, tiptoe, stalk, float, glide, *and* melt; *examples of verbs for heavy movements include* rock, stomp, stamp, pounce, crash, *or* explode.

To Have

Chart paper and markers

To Do

- The children demonstrate different light and heavy movements. Make sure to alternate the *light* and *heavy* verbs.
- Write the words on chart paper and post it for children to see.

More to Do

- The words suggested above lend themselves to movement with the whole body. You can also contrast words associated with the hands and arms. For example, *light* words could include *tap, pat, stroke,* and *flutter. Heavy* words could include *pound, poke, chop,* and *flap.*

- Use a hand drum or a tambourine to signal changes from one movement to another. For instance, bang on the drum loudly to suggest stomping and tap on it lightly to suggest tiptoeing.

"Put Your Little Foot" from Kimbo's *Baby Face* calls for tiptoeing and stomping.

Reinforces understanding of verbs and opposites

Slow and Fast Words in Action

This activity uses verbs that indicate slow movements (such as stomp, trudge, meander, *and* sneak*) and fast movements (such as* hurry, fly, run, dash, *and* scurry*).*

To Have

Chart paper and markers (optional)

To Do

- Have the children demonstrate different *slow* and *fast* words, alternating between the two.
- Post a list of the words on chart paper, if desired.

SLOWLY WALKING

RUNNING

Slow Loris by Alexis Deacon is about a lemur that does everything very slowly during the day. At night while the other animals sleep, Loris's actions are fast!

All About Adjectives

This activity teaches children about adjectives (descriptive words). Whether or not you use the word adjective, *the children will better comprehend these descriptive words as they demonstrate them physically.*

To Have

● List of the words you want to explore. Adjectives that lend themselves to demonstrating include:

- strong
- light
- graceful
- forceful
- smooth
- droopy
- gentle
- floppy
- careful
- enormous
- tiny
- excited

To Do

● Talk to the children about the meaning of the words you have chosen.
● Call out one word at a time, inviting the children to demonstrate each word.

Read *The Teeny-Tiny Woman* by Paul Galdone. Ask the children to act out the story. Brian P. Cleary's *Hairy, Scary, Ordinary: What Is an Adjective?* is another good resource for reading and acting out adjectives.

Reinforces an understanding of adverbs

All About Adverbs

Children this age are too young to understand that adverbs modify verbs. However, they will delight in demonstrating the words; as a result, adverbs will have much greater relevance to them.

To Have

No materials needed

To Do

- Talk to the children about any words that you feel require explanation, then challenge them to do the following:

  - Walk lightly.
  - Walk heavily.
  - Walk slowly.
  - Walk quickly.
  - Stomp loudly.
  - Tiptoe quietly.
  - Walk angrily.
  - Walk proudly.
  - Move swiftly.
  - Move tiredly.
  - Walk crookedly.
  - Walk sadly.
  - Walk happily.

Dearly, Nearly, Insincerely: What Is an Adverb? by Brian P. Clearly and *Up, Up and Away: A Book About Adverbs* by Ruth Heller are two good books about adverbs.

Happy Endings

The children may be too young to understand suffixes, but they can show you the meanings of the same word with different endings.

To Have

A list of words you want to explore with the children

To Do

- A suffix is a letter or group of letters that is added to the end of a word to form another word.
- Ask the children to demonstrate the different meanings of the following sets of words that all begin with the same letters but end differently:

  - scared/scary
  - squeezing/squeezed
  - collapsed/collapsing
  - long/longer
  - happy/happiest

Prefixes and Suffixes by Ann Heinrichs is appropriate for children ages 4 to 8.

Reading   95

Promotes word comprehension and the ability to make meaning of the text

Retell Me a Story

Text retelling is the process of retelling a story through varying methods. It helps you gauge the children's progress in word comprehension and in making meaning (understanding the essence of the story). Retelling is done after children listen to or read a story. One of the methods for retelling is acting out the story.

To Have

A short book with a simple plot that the children are already familiar with. Rowen (1982, p. 43) suggests the following criteria for determining whether a story is appropriate for dramatization:

1. The story must have action.
2. The plot must include changes in emotion.
3. Only two or three of the story's characters should be involved in the same action.
4. These characters should have different personality traits.

To Do

- Read the book to the children.
- After reading the story, have the children take turns acting it out from beginning to end!

The Little Engine That Could by Watty Piper and *Strega Nona* by Tomie dePaola are good examples of books to use for dramatization.

CHAPTER 4

Writing

Reading and writing should be considered a developmental continuum; one leads to the other, but not necessarily in a precise sequence (Neuman & Roskos, 2005).

Spatial orientation—whether it concerns the way a *b* as opposed to a *d* faces, or the movement from top to bottom and left to right—is fundamental to reading and to writing. Many of the activities in the previous chapter involved *directionality*, which prepares children for writing, as well. Additional activities addressing spatial orientation can be found in this chapter.

You will also find activities promoting eye-hand coordination, hand and finger strengthening, and the ability to replicate physically what the eyes see, all necessary to the mechanical aspects of writing. However, writing is not only about mechanical aspects; it is also a creative process. Some of the activities in this chapter foster self-expression, creativity, and a love of language.

As in Chapter 3: Reading, the activities in this chapter are more focused on pre-writing skills than on actual writing. The abilities to read and to write occur on a child's own timetable. When the time comes for children to write, they will be ready!

Develops the ability to replicate physically what the eyes see

Follow the Leader

The ability to replicate physically what the eyes see is essential for writing. This is what children do when they make their initial attempts at copying letters from a poster, chalkboard, or book. Follow the Leader is a fun, familiar way for children to practice this skill.

To Have

No materials needed

To Do

● Lead the children around the room performing whatever locomotor (traveling) skills, such as walking, marching, hopping, and skipping, they can all execute successfully.

● Vary your tempo (slow, fast, and various speeds in between), pathways (straight, curved, and zigzag), force (light, strong, and the range from light to strong), and levels (high, low, and in between).

More to Do

● When the children are ready for the responsibility, let them take turns leading.

● As you lead the group, occasionally call out the name of one of the children. Ask that child to break away from the line, leading everyone behind him. This makes the game a listening activity, as well.

● Add the element of rhythm to the game by playing a recording of a march and making a parade.

You can use the classics, such as the marches of John Philip Sousa or pieces written especially for children such as those found on Hap Palmer's *Mod Marches*.

Accompany this activity with one of several books entitled *Follow the Leader*, by authors including Emma Chichester Clark, Erica Silverman, and Miela Ford.

The Mirror Game

This activity offers additional practice replicating physically what the eyes see (see previous activity, Follow the Leader). In this activity, children stay in one place rather than traveling around the room.

To Have

No materials needed

To Do

- Stand facing the children so they can all see you. Explain that you are going to perform certain actions and they are going to pretend to be your mirror reflection.
- Challenge them to do exactly what you do as you do it. Possible actions include:

  - raising and lowering an arm
  - nodding the head
  - bending and straightening the knees
  - bending at the waist and then straightening
  - lifting and lowering a leg
  - tilting to the side and returning to an upright position
  - making a funny face

More to Do

- When the children are able to work together cooperatively, they can play this game in pairs, alternating between leading and reflecting.

"The Mirror Game" on Jill Gallina's *Hand Jivin'* explores this concept. To make sure it continues to be an exercise in replication, have the children do the actions called for in the lyrics to this song. Later, make it more of an active listening experience by letting the children respond on their own.

Strengthens hands and fingers and promotes word comprehension

Ten Little Fingers

Strong hands and fingers are important for writing. This activity strengthens hands and fingers as it enhances the children's vocabulary by reinforcing understanding of such words as tight, wide, together, high, low, *and* quietly.

To Have

No materials needed

To Do

- Read the following poem to the children.
- Encourage them to move their fingers as the words tell them to.

I have ten little fingers,
And they all belong to me.
I can make them do things.
Would you like to see?
I can shut them up tight
Or open them wide.
I can put them together
Or make them all hide.
I can make them jump high.
I can make them jump low.
I can fold them quietly
And hold them just so!

Read the board book *Ten Little Fingers* by Annie Kubler. You will also find this nursery rhyme in *Ten Little Fingers: 100 Number Rhymes for Young Children* by Louise Binder Scott.

Open and Close

With fewer opportunities to swing across monkey bars or climb trees, today's children need as many hand-strengthening activities as we can provide for them. This simple activity is good for strengthening the muscles of the hands.

To Have

No materials needed

To Do

- Lead the children in opening and closing their hands at varying tempos, alternately stretching fingers to their limit and then clenching fists tightly!
- Use the words *open* and *close* to reinforce these opposite verbs.

More to Do

- Provide each child with a small rubber ball to squeeze and release. This strengthens hand and finger muscles.

Improves hand strength and fine motor coordination

Counting Fingers

This activity requires a lot of repetition and offers the added bonus of reinforcing counting and sequencing skills.

To Have

No materials needed

To Do

- Have the children curl their hands into loose fists. As you count (very slowly at first!) from one to ten, have them uncurl one finger at a time.
- Reverse, counting backward from ten to one, with the children curling one finger at a time back into the palms of their hands.

For a musical experience counting on fingers, play "I Have Ten Little Fingers" from *Fingerplays and Footplays* by Rosemary Hallum and Henry Buzz Glass, and "I Can Count to Ten" on Maryann "Mar" Harman's *Playing and Learning with Music.*

In *Hand, Hand, Fingers, Thumb* by Al Perkins, silly monkeys explain hands, fingers, and thumbs to beginning readers.

Finger Fun

Children get a kick out of this simple activity.

To Have

No materials needed

To Do

- As you call out *pointer, middle, ring,* or *pinky,* have the children touch their corresponding finger with the thumb on that hand.
- Vary the tempo and order in which you call out the words.
- Practice with one hand at a time and then both hands together.

More to Do

- As you call out *thumb, pointer, middle, ring,* or *pinky* mixing up the order and tempo, have the children tap the corresponding digits on a table, their lap, or on the floor in front of them.

Ambrose Brazelton's *Clap, Snap, and Tap* and Jill Gallina's *Hand Jivin'* offer many rhythmic hand movements.

Strengthens fingers

Finger Push-Ups

The children are probably familiar with the push-ups people do to keep fit, but they may not be aware that fingers can also do push-ups!

To Have

Hand drum (optional)

To Do

- The children touch the tips of the fingers and thumb on one hand to the tips of the fingers and thumb on the other hand.
- They alternately stretch and bend (lengthen and shorten) the fingers without breaking contact between them.
- You might accompany this exercise with a drum beat, or a hand clap, or by calling out, "Stretch and bend!"

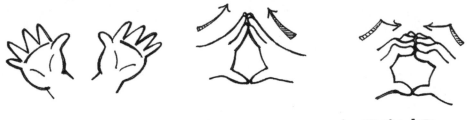

STRETCH and BEND

More to Do

- When you feel the children are strong enough, ask them to stand facing a wall, about a foot away from it. With elbows bent by their sides, they lean forward at an angle and touch the wall with the tips of their fingers. They then do "push-ups" by alternately extending and bending their fingers.

Ready Wrists

Fingers are not the only body parts that must be strong for writing. Strong wrists are also important for manipulating writing implements.

To Have

No materials needed

To Do

- Have the children sit with their arms extended in front of them, palms of the hands facing away from them. As you chant *front* and *back*, have the children alternately turn only their hands toward and then away from themselves.

More to Do

- Play the same game with palms facing down. Using their wrists, the children turn their hands so the palms are *up* and then *down*.
- Invite the children to show you how they would use their hands if they were:

  - using a screwdriver
  - twisting the lid off a jar
  - turning a water faucet on and off
  - waving goodbye

- Ask the children to pretend to draw small circles in the air in front of them, moving only their hands.
- Have the children show you how windshield wipers move from side to side using only their hands.

Strengthens hands and promotes word comprehension

Hands in Action

This activity gives the hands a workout and expands vocabulary.

To Have

No materials needed

To Do

● Have the children demonstrate the following actions using only their hands. Discuss the meaning of each word and use each in a sentence to help with comprehension:

• clap, pat, tap, wring, sew, stroke, wave, beckon, pinch, pluck, strum, fan

More to Do

● Have the children demonstrate how their hands would "say" the following:

"Hello."
"Come here."
"Go away."
"I'm scared."
"I'm cold."
"I'm worried."
"I'm hungry."
"I'm hot."
"Goodbye."

Hands Are Not for Hitting by Martine Agassi explores other uses for hands, such as waving, drawing, and making music.

What's My Line?

Letters consist of vertical, horizontal, diagonal, crossed, curving, and zigzagging lines. This activity introduces some of these lines to the children and reinforces others.

To Have

Large letters, both upper- and lowercase, posted for the children to see

To Do

- Talk to the children about each of the kinds of lines that comprise letters.
- Point out, for example, the horizontal line in an uppercase *A*, or the two diagonal lines creating the point in an uppercase *A*, and ask the children to replicate the line with their body or with individual body parts.

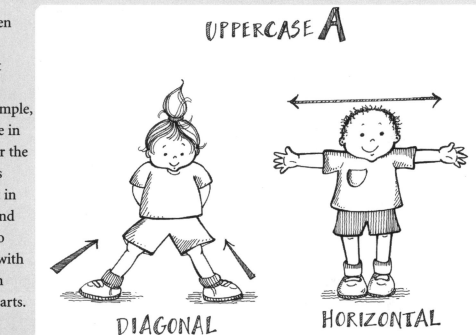

UPPERCASE A

DIAGONAL   HORIZONTAL

More to Do

- Challenge the children to create various lines in groups of two or three.
- Have the children find examples of different lines throughout the room. For instance, a flagpole creates a vertical line. Once the children have made a discovery, ask them to replicate it with their body.
- Create various lines on the floor with masking tape. Have the children move along the lines using different locomotor skills, such as walking or creeping (moving on hands and knees).

Reinforces letter recognition and the ability to physically replicate what the eyes see

Follow That Letter

Like All About the Alphabet (page 77), this activity helps imprint the straight and curving lines of letters on both the mind and body.

To Have

Several jump ropes

To Do

- In a few places on the floor make the same letter shape with several jump ropes.
- Divide the children into groups equal to the number of ropes you have used.
- Have the children get into single file lines and, one at a time, "trace" the pattern of the letter with a designated locomotor skill (for example, walking, jogging, jumping, galloping, hopping, or skipping).
- Reshape the ropes to form a different letter and assign a new locomotor skill and repeat the activity.

SKIPPING the LETTER "C"

More to Do

- Eventually add adjectives to the game. For example, you might invite the children to jog *slowly*, walk *lightly*, jump *heavily*, or gallop *quickly* along the letter.
- Put large cutout letters on the floor throughout the room. Specify a locomotor skill (such as jumping) for children to do on the way to a designated letter. At your signal, ask the children to move to the letter's location on the floor and trace the shape of the letter with a finger of their writing hand.

"Bend It, Twist It, Turn It," on Brenda Colgate's *Silly Willy's Pre-Jump Rope Skills* has children create letters with jump ropes.

Coordinating Hand and Eye

Tracking and trying to catch a falling chiffon scarf is a wonderful way to foster eye-hand coordination, a critical component of learning how to write. Chiffon scarves fall slowly, so the children have a good chance of experiencing success!

To Have

One chiffon scarf (or paper towel square) per child

To Do

- Spread the children throughout the area so they are unlikely to bump into one another.
- Have the children throw their scarves into the air as high as possible and try to catch them before they land on the floor.

More to Do

- As the children become more accomplished at this, ask them to:

  - Turn around once while the scarf is still in the air.
  - Clap their hands while the scarf is still in the air. How many claps can they get in before the scarf touches the ground?
  - Try tossing two scarves into the air and catching them both before they touch the ground.

"Magic Scarf" on Hap Palmer's *Can Cockatoos Count by Twos?* offers creative ways for children to use scarves to develop eye-hand coordination.

Promotes eye-hand coordination

Coordinating Hand and Eye II

Volleying (striking an object in an upward direction) is another great way to develop eye-hand coordination. The children will have no idea that this game has anything to do with writing. They will just know they are having fun!

To Have

One medium to large inflated balloon per child

To Do

- Encourage the children to practice hitting their balloons upward and forward with both hands.
- When they are experiencing more success than failure, challenge them to *volley* with just one (the preferred) hand.
- Finally, challenge them to try volleying with their non-preferred hand.

More to Do

- Have the children work together in pairs to keep a balloon in the air. For an added challenge, neither partner is allowed to touch the balloon twice in a row!
- Eye-hand coordination is made even more challenging when an implement, such as a paddle, is used to volley an object away from the body. When the children are ready for a greater challenge, give each child a paddle with which to volley the balloon.

Recordings that help develop eye-hand coordination include *Perceptual Motor Rhythm Games* and *Motor Fitness Rhythm Games*, both by Jack Capon and Rosemary Hallum, and *Rhythm Stick Activities* by Henry Buzz Glass and Rosemary Hallum.

Skywriting

When there is no permanent product such as written letters required to demonstrate whether they have gotten it right or wrong, children feel a lot less pressure to write "correctly." Pretending to write in the air is fun!

To Have

Alphabet chart (optional)

To Do

- If available, hang an alphabet chart where children can see it.
- Ask the children to imagine that the air in front of them is a giant chalkboard and that they have a big piece of chalk in their writing hand.
- Have them choose letters of the alphabet (upper- or lowercase) and "write" them on the "chalkboard." They should begin by making their letters as large as possible.

More to Do

- Encourage the children to reduce the size of the letters gradually.
- Have one child at a time write a letter in the air, and ask the rest of the class to guess the letter.
- Invite the children to write with other body parts: their elbows, noses, the tops of their heads, or even their belly buttons! Children love this activity, particularly the belly button challenge!
- If you have chiffon scarves or ribbon wands, invite the children to use them like chalk or paintbrushes to write letters in the air. Because they can see the pathways created by the scarves or ribbons, the pathways in the air become visible and, therefore, less abstract. The children enjoy these props!

A "T" USING A HEAD

DOWN

UP

LEAN LEFT   LEAN RIGHT

Promotes directionality, cross-lateral movement, and pre-writing practice

Floor Writing

This activity provides more practice moving from left to right, crossing the midline, and experiencing the straight and curving lines of letters.

To Have

Alphabet chart (optional)

To Do

- Post an alphabet chart, if available, for children to refer to.
- Ask the children to imagine that the floor in front of them is a big piece of paper and that they have chalk, paint, or ink on the big toe of one foot.
- Have the children use their toes to "write" lower- or uppercase letters on the floor.

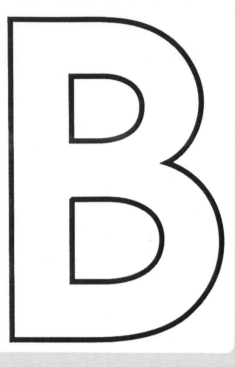

More to Do

- Accompanying this activity with various styles of music changes the way the children create their letters. Classical and New Age pieces will inspire long, smooth strokes, while rock, pop, and jazz will inspire short, staccato movements.

Above, Below, and On

Children need a clear understanding of the words above, below, *and* on *before they can succeed in writing letters and words on lined paper. These are the three positions on which all or parts of their letters will be placed in relation to the lines on the paper.*

To Have

One jump rope per child

To Do

- Each child places his rope flat on the floor in a straight horizontal line.
- Call out "above," "below," or "on," indicating where the children should stand in relation to the line. Call out each word in various orders and tempos!

More to Do

- If your group is small enough and you have a long enough rope, there is a similar activity for children standing side by side. You will either have to secure the rope on both ends or assign two children to hold the ends. The rope should be at waist height, with the children standing behind it. When you call out *above*, the children reach their arms over the top of the rope. When you call out *below*, they put their arms below the rope. And when you call out *on*, they put their hands on the rope.

Introduces directionality and laterality

The Hokey Pokey

This traditional favorite song and dance provides experience with left and right.

To Have

Recording of "The Hokey Pokey"

To Do

- First teach the lyrics without the music, indicating to the children their left and right hands and feet.
- When they are familiar enough with the words and the accompanying actions, play the song and do the dance.

You can find a recording of "The Hokey Pokey" on *Children's All-Time Rhythm Favorites.*

The Hokey Pokey is a Wee Sing board book that you can read as a story or use to sing along with.

Hello, Kitty

Once the children have had ample experience forming letters with their bodies, they can start to create words.

To Have

No materials needed

To Do

- Working in small groups, the children use their bodies to form letters that spell out short words, such as "hi" and "cat."

More to Do

- Have one group at a time spell out a word, and the rest of the children guess the word.

Promotes spatial awareness

Mind Your Ps and Qs

Spatial orientation is an essential component of writing. We write from left to right across the page and from the top of the page to the bottom. Some letters, such as lowercase b and d, consist of the same components—a straight line with a curved line at the bottom—but face in different directions! A lowercase p and an uppercase P are identical except that the line on the lowercase letter is found below the line on the page and the line on the uppercase letter is found above the line. This activity reinforces the spatial awareness needed to recognize these differences and helps imprint it on the children's bodies and minds.

To Have

Chart paper and markers or alphabet chart

To Do

- Post a chart of lower- and uppercase letters, or make one using chart paper and markers.
- Show the children a lowercase *t* and an uppercase *T*, and point out that the lines are the same. On the lowercase *t*, however, the horizontal line crosses the vertical line; on the uppercase *T*, the line sits on top.
- Ask the children to take on the shape of each letter, repeating them several times.
- Show the children a lowercase *b* and ask them to take on its shape with their bodies or body parts.
- Do the same with the letter *d*. Repeat this several times.
- Continue with the upper- and lowercase *p*, and with the letters *p* and *q*.

More to Do

- Ask the children to demonstrate the difference between a lowercase *g* and a lowercase *q*.

Go with the Flow

Children need to understand the functions of punctuation marks. This fun activity introduces the use of the period, the comma, and the question mark.

To Have

Three large index cards and markers

To Do

- Draw a period on one card, a comma on another card, and a question mark on a third card. Display the cards and discuss each mark.
- At your signal, ask the children to begin walking around the room.
- When you hold up the card with the period and say "period," the children come to a complete stop.
- When you hold up the question mark card and say "question mark," the children stop and shrug their shoulders.
- When you hold up the comma card and say "comma," the children pause momentarily and then continue walking.

More to Do

- When the children recognize these three punctuation marks on their own, stop naming them as you hold up their cards.
- Use this opportunity to practice a variety of locomotor skills. Instead of walking, the children can jog lightly, jump, hop, gallop, or skip.

Use the CD/cassette/book combo called *Grammar and Punctuation Songs* for ages 4 to 8 for additional punctuation experiences.

Read *Punctuation Takes a Vacation* by Robin Pulver.

Introduces phrases and sentences

Go with the Flow II

Linking movements to form sequences is not that different from linking words to form phrases and sentences. The best components must be used to ensure ease of flow.

To Have

No materials needed

To Do

- Start slowly, asking the children to combine steps with jumps.
- Then ask them to combine any two or three locomotor or nonlocomotor skills, in any order. Possible combinations include the following:

  - jump-turn
  - jump-stretch
  - jump-stretch-turn
  - run-leap
  - run-leap-sway
  - skip-swing
  - skip-swing-stretch

More to Do

- For a greater challenge, the children can incorporate punctuation into their sequences, with a pause representing a comma and a full stop representing a period. A sample sequence would be jump-pause-stretch-stop.

If You're Happy and You Know It

The process of writing is not only about the mechanics involved; it also entails creating. The next several activities will enhance the children's creative and critical-thinking skills as they apply to writing.

To Have

No materials needed

To Do

- Once the children can sing the song and perform the motions in the traditional way ("If you're happy and you know it, clap your hands"), have them suggest other emotions.
- Which actions would go along with those feelings? For example, "If you're frightened and you know it, hide your eyes."

A number of books share the title of this song, among them: a sing-along action book by Jane Cabrera, a pop-up version by David Carter, and a third selection by Jan Ormerod.

Develops creative writing, enunciation, and word comprehension; enhances vocabulary

Row, Row, Row Your Boat

Singing this song gives children a chance to practice the /r/ sound and reinforces comprehension of words such as gently *and* merrily. *Creating substitutions for the original lyrics (and the accompanying action suggested below) stimulates children's creativity and enhances their vocabulary.*

To Have

No materials needed

To Do

- Discuss the meaning of the lyrics with the children and demonstrate a rowing action for them.
- Invite them to sing while they "row" back and forth across the room.
- Ask the children to suggest other vehicles that could be substituted for the rowboat and the appropriate accompanying actions (for example, paddling a canoe or kayak, or driving the car). If the children come up with actions unrelated to being on the water, such as "Drive, drive, drive your car," brainstorm how to also change the second and fourth lines of the song.

Row, row, row your boat
Gently down the stream.
Merrily, merrily, merrily, merrily,
Life is but a dream.

MOVING ARMS FORWARD and BACKWARD (ROWING)

MOVING A STEERING WHEEL

You will find a recorded version of this song on Bob McGrath's *Songs and Games for Toddlers.*

Row, Row, Row Your Boat by Iza Trapani is accompanied by a CD on which the words are both sung and read. Pippa Goodhart has created a version in which a girl, a boy, and a toy rabbit reenact the traditional song.

A–Marching We Will Go

This activity is based on the same premise as the two previous activities (pages 119 and 120): substituting words and actions to stimulate the imagination and enhance vocabulary. Additionally, marching is a cross-lateral experience!

To Have

No materials needed

To Do

- Teach the children the following song, sung to the tune of "Farmer in the Dell":

  A-marching we will go,
  A-marching we will go,
  Heigh, ho, the derry-o,
  A-marching we will go.

- The children sing and march at the same time. Explain to the children that "march" is an action word.
- Once they have had a chance to experience this verse, ask them to think of other action words to substitute.

Promotes understanding of story structure

What Comes Next?

Predicting what comes next in a story "helps readers to stay focused on content and to explore the ways in which authors structure their writing" (Owocki, 2001, p. 55).

To Have

A book or story with a predictable plot, such as:

- *The Gigantic Turnip* by Aleksei Tolstoy
- "The Gingerbread Man" (traditional)
- *If You Give a Mouse a Cookie* by Laura Joffe Numeroff
- *The Napping House* by Audrey Wood
- "The Three Bears" (traditional)
- *Why Mosquitoes Buzz in People's Ears* by Verna Aardema

To Do

- Read the story aloud to the children, stopping occasionally to ask them what they think happens next. Acknowledge all of their ideas and then invite them to demonstrate their predictions physically.
- Before you reach the conclusion of the book, stop again and ask the children how they think the story ends.

Build a Story

Creating stories takes a vivid imagination and a sense of adventure. Young children have both in abundance! This activity calls on children to use both, and it enhances their vocabularies.

To Have

No materials needed

To Do

- Sit with the children in a circle and start a story with one line; for example, "Once upon a time, a little boy and girl …"
- Ask the child to your right or left to continue the story from there, contributing no more than two sentences.
- Continue the process all the way around the circle with each child adding to the story.
- By the time the story comes back to you, it should be concluded. If it doesn't have what the children feel is a satisfactory ending, supply one yourself!

Promotes creative writing and love of language

Nonsense!

Children love nonsense words, as they appeal to their silly sense of humor. This activity exposes them to nonsense words and gives them the opportunity to make up some of their own!

To Have

No materials needed

To Do

- Ask each child to make up a word they have never heard before and to decide what it means. Ask the children, one at a time, to speak and then demonstrate their word.

- Have the rest of the children repeat the word and try to guess its meaning! For example, a child might make up a word like "woogly" and then depict it as a combination of wiggly and wobbly. Be prepared for silly words that make a lot less sense!

For more exploration of nonsense and nonsense words, share Stoo Hample's *The Silly Book.*

Glossary

Alliteration: A string of words with the same beginning sound.

Auditory discrimination: The ability to differentiate among sounds.

Auditory perception: The ability to hear likenesses and differences in sounds.

Auditory processing: The ability to sort out what is heard.

Auditory sequential memory: The ability to hear and recall a series of words, sounds, or instructions.

Cross-lateral movement: Movement in which the limbs move in opposition. For example, when crawling, the right arm and left leg or the left arm and right leg move simultaneously.

Crossing the midline: Reaching across the invisible line that runs from the head to the toes and divides the body into left and right halves.

Decoding: The ability to sound out letters.

Directionality: Awareness of directions in space; for example, up, down, right, and left.

Laterality: Understanding that the body is divided into left and right halves.

Locomotor skills: Movements like walking and running that transport the body as a whole from one point to another.

Onomatopoeia: The term used to describe words that sound like what they mean.

Phonemic awareness: Awareness that language is broken down into small units called phonemes, which correspond to letters of the alphabet.

Phonological awareness: Appreciation for the sounds and meaning of spoken words.

Print awareness: Recognition of the conventions and characteristics of a written language.

Speech pattern: Speech characteristics of an individual; for example, speaking in rhymes, stuttering, or speaking rapidly.

Suffixes: A letter or group of letters added to the end of a word to form another word.

Syllable: A unit of spoken language.

Temporal awareness: Awareness of rhythm that helps individuals internalize the rhythm of literary works.

Text retelling: Process of retelling a story through various methods.

References

Block, B.A. (2001). Literacy through movement: An organizational approach. *Journal of Physical Education, Recreation & Dance*, 72(1), 39-48.

California Department of Education. (1999). *First class: A guide for primary education, preschool, kindergarten, and first grade.* Sacramento CA: California Department of Education.

Corso, M. (1993). Is developmentally appropriate physical education the answer to children's school readiness? *Colorado Journal of Health, Physical Education, Recreation, and Dance*, 19(2), 6-7.

Coulter, D. (1995). Music and the making of the mind. *Early Childhood Connections: The Journal of Music- and Movement-Based Learning*, 1, 22-26.

Dennison, P., & Dennison, G. (1989). *Brain gym (Teacher's edition).* Ventura CA: Edu-Kinesthetics.

Fauth, B. (1990). Linking the visual arts with drama, movement, and dance for the young child. In W.J. Stinson, (ed), *Moving and learning for the young child* (pp. 159-187). Reston VA: American Alliance for Health, Physical Education, Recreation, and Dance.

Gardner, H. (1993). *Frames of mind: The theory of multiple intelligences.* New York: Basic Books.

Hannaford, C. (1995). *Smart moves: Why learning isn't all in your head.* Arlington VA: Great Ocean.

Isenberg, J.P., & Jalongo, M.R. (2002). *Creative expression and play in the early childhood curriculum.* New York: Merrill.

Jaques-Dalcroze, E. (1931). *Eurhythmics, art, and education* (F. Rothwell, Trans.; C. Cox, Ed.). New York: A. S. Barnes.

Jensen, E. (2001). *Arts with the brain in mind.* Alexandria VA: Association for Supervision and Curriculum Development.

Machado, J.M. (2003). *Early childhood experiences in language arts, 7th ed.* Clifton Park NY: Delmar.

Minton, S. (2003). Using movement to teach academics: An outline for success. *Journal of Physical Education, Recreation & Dance*, 74(2), 36-40.

Neuman, S.B., & Roskos, K. (2005). Whatever happened to developmentally appropriate practice in early literacy? *Young Children*, 60(4), 22-26.

Olds, A. R. (1994). From cartwheels to caterpillars: Children's need to move indoors and out. *Early Childhood Exchange*, 32-36.

Orlick, T. (1978). *The cooperative sports and games book: Challenge without competition.* New York: Pantheon.

Owocki, G. (2001). *Make way for literacy!* Portsmouth NH: Heinemann & Washington DC: NAEYC.

Pinnell, G.S. (1999). Word solving. In I. Fountas & G. S. Pinnell (Eds.), *Voices on word matters: Learning about phonics and spelling in the literacy classroom* (pp. 151-186). Portsmouth NH: Heinemann.

Raines, S.C., & Canady, R.J. (1990). *The whole language kindergarten.* New York: Teachers College.

Rowen, B. (1982). *Learning through movement.* New York: Teacher's College.

Sawyer, W.E., & Sawyer, J.C. (1993). *Integrated language arts for emerging literacy.* Clifton Park NY: Delmar.

Index of Literacy Skills

Index of Children's Books

Index

big science
for little hands

Curious
Crayons
early childhood science in living color

teacher's guide

Art Credits

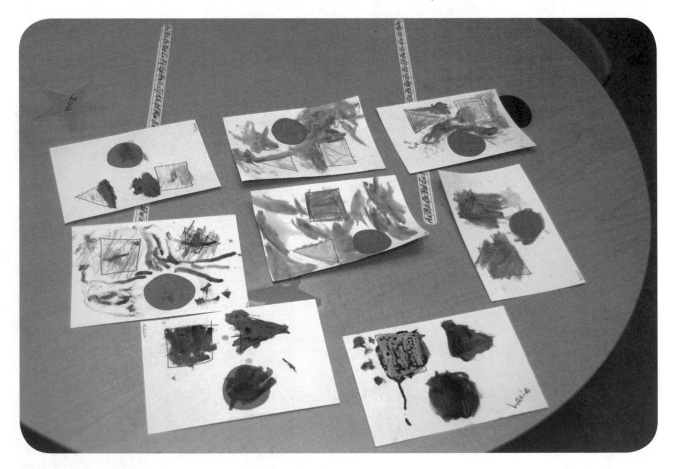

Curious Crayons

early childhood science in living color

Editor

Mickey Sarquis, Director
Center for Chemistry Education and Terrific Science Programs
Miami University, Middletown, OH

Contributing Authors

Ann Veith, Rosedale Elementary School (retired), Middletown, OH
Beverly Kutsunai, Kamehameha Elementary School, Honolulu, HI
Lynn Hogue, Center for Chemistry Education, Miami University,
   Middletown, OH

Terrific Science Press
Miami University Middletown
Middletown, Ohio

teacher's guide

Terrific Science Press
Miami University Middletown
4200 East University Boulevard
Middletown, OH 45042
513/727-3269
cce@muohio.edu
www.terrificscience.org

10 9 8 7 6 5 4 3 2 1

This monograph is intended for use by teachers and properly supervised children. The safety reminders associated with experiments and activities in this publication have been compiled from sources believed to be reliable and to represent the best opinions on the subject as of the date of publication. No warranty, guarantee, or representation is made by the authors or by Terrific Science Press as to the correctness or sufficiency of any information herein. Neither the authors nor the publisher assume any responsibility or liability for the use of the information herein, nor can it be assumed that all necessary warnings and precautionary measures are contained in this publication. Other or additional information or measures may be required or desirable because of particular or exceptional conditions or circumstances.

ISBN: 978-1-883822-54-5

This material is based upon work supported by the **Ohio Board of Regents** (Grant Number 06-25). Any opinions, findings, and conclusions or recommendations expressed in this material are those of the authors and do not necessarily reflect the views of the funding agency.